DAVID NELIGAN

It was David Neligan who gave h_____ ___ *soubriquet* "The Spy in the Castle". When his account of his work for Michael Collins was published in 1968 it was greeted as a significant contribution to the history of the troubled 1916-1921 period in Ireland. But the story which it told is only a part of his life, spanning just a few years of the decade and a half over which he was centrally involved in the evolution of a new Ireland. The great pity is that he did not publish a second and perhaps even a third book, offering his account of his participation in the Civil War and the turbulent years in which he was head of the security and intelligence service of the Irish Free State.

He was born in Templeglantine, Co Limerick in 1899, where his parents were national school teachers. At 18 years of age he decided to become a policeman, taking a path which was customary for many a young Irish countryman with the foundations of a good education and a bit of ambition. His career began in the Dublin Metropolitan Police, patrolling the streets of the capital, unarmed, in the days before the Irish War of Independence. He graduated relatively quickly to the detective branch and it was in his role as a member of "G" Division (the DMP's uniformed divisions ran from "A" to "F") that he found himself uniquely placed to play a key role in Collins's intelligence war against the British.

His exploits in assisting Collins are the subject of this book. It tells an extraordinary tale of nerve and bluff. From within the centre of the British security machine he fed information to Collins, enabling the IRA to stay ahead of its enemies in intelligence matters at virtually all times throughout the conflict. Neligan was one of a number of Irish-born members of the detective branch operating for Collins over this period. The two others best known, Eamonn "Ned" Broy and James McNamara, also come into this narrative. McNamara was to die tragically at a young age. Broy, on the other hand, was to become Neligan's nemesis later in their careers. In his epic film *Michael Collins,* director Neil Jordan conflated the personalities and exploits of all three detectives into one "Ned Broy" character.

When the War of Independence ended the Civil War began. The Irish Free State had to quickly raise a regular army and David Neligan, his role as a double agent never having been uncovered by the British, transferred to the National Army with the rank of colonel.

He was a tough soldier, assigned to Kerry where the fighting against anti-Treaty forces was bloody and dirty. Men under his command were involved in actions - reprisals perhaps - which led to the deaths of helpless prisoners. Anti-Treaty forces had rigged roadblocks with booby-trapped mines which killed several Free State soldiers as they endeavoured to clear them. The Free State forces henceforth decided that prisoners would be used to clear barricades. In two incidents, at Ballyseedy and Countess Bridge, mines exploded killing and maiming prisoners.

Neligan's name was invariably linked to these incidents in anti-Treaty accounts of the Kerry fighting. The extent to which he might or might not have been involved has never been publicly documented. But it is certain that his subsequent career gave every incentive to the opponents of the Treaty to blacken his reputation. He led the men of Oriel House, an *ad hoc* assemblage of gunmen operating as a secret police on behalf of the Provisional Government. After Kerry he served as Director of Intelligence until the end of 1923. He then returned to the Dublin Metropolitan Police, not as a constable but as a chief superintendent. A new unarmed police force, the Garda Siochana, was formed in 1922 and was given responsibility for law and order outside the Dublin Metropolitan Area. When it was amalgamated with the DMP in 1925 Neligan was transferred, still with the rank of chief superintendent to take command of a new, State-wide, armed detective branch. Broy, who had also resumed his police career, became chief superintendent of the newly-designated Dublin Metropolitan Division. Neligan was given the task of pacifying those elements throughout the State which still refused to come to terms with the new order.

It was not an easy task. He established the Special Branch (it was known universally as the S-Branch) throughout the State. Small groups of two and three detectives, often ex-IRA men, were dotted here and there. They were armed and mobile whereas the uniformed Garda Siochana was unarmed and without efficient transport or communications systems. The S-Branch met with vigorous resistance from unreconstructed republicans who resolved to continue the struggle against the Free State or, in some instances, by opportunists from both sides who had simply turned to crime. Some S-Branch men died. Many were wounded or injured. But Neligan's men gradually got the upper-hand, albeit with the aid of stern emergency powers and a not-too-scrupulous approach to the policeman's powers at law.

They were turbulent years. Neligan was seldom directly involved in operations. He directed his network from the Crime Branch at Garda Headquarters at the Phoenix Park Depot. He reported to Commissioner Eoin O'Duffy but had direct access to the Minister for Justice and, as necessary, to the head of the Government, William T Cosgrave. His influence was considerable. His estimation of the public mood and of the state of crime and subversion formed the basis of the Government's day to day security policy. He was responsible for preparing, at intervals, the exotically-entitled "Confidential Report to the Government on Organisations and Persons Inimical to the State".

In 1927 members of the IRA assassinated the Minister for Justice, Kevin O'Higgins. It was a hammer-blow to the security forces and it was a serious reverse for Neligan's reputation. Some who knew him said that after the death of O'Higgins he never fully regained the self-confidence and assertiveness of his earlier years.

By the early 1930s, Neligan could look at the map on the wall of his office at the Phoenix Park Garda headquarters and reassure himself that only a few rural districts, principally in the west, the south and along the border, still presented overt problems to his detective force. But the outer appearances of tranquillity concealed continuing, deep resistance to the Treaty and gathering political hostility to the government which had overseen its installation as the basis of governance. In 1932 the Cosgrave government was swept from power and a new Fianna Fail administration, under Eamon de Valera came to office. Among the earliest casualties, in career terms, were the Commissioner, Eoin O'Duffy and Neligan himself. Neligan was relegated to an obscure post in another Government department and worked out his service there. His replacement at the Special Branch was Eamon Broy who was shortly afterwards appointed Commissioner in succession to O'Duffy.

In 1973 while researching for a post-graduate thesis, I called and introduced myself to David Neligan, then in his '70s and living quietly in retirement at Booterstown, on the south Dublin coastline. He received me courteously and we spent a succession of evenings drinking tea in his drawing room while I probed him on the security policy of the Free State Government. As our meetings progressed he became more relaxed and forthright in his recollections and I believe I can say we got on well.

He had a formidable recall of detail. I was repeatedly stuck at the accuracy of names, streets, even house-numbers when he recounted incidents which had occurred fifty years earlier.

I also recall his modesty in describing his work for Collins. He had a humourous, self-deprecatory way of telling a story or detailing some operation in which he might have been involved. He had a strong sense of humanity and I recall his desire in all of his narratives to put an end to old accounts. He spoke of men who had lost their lives through his actions or the actions of those who worked under his command, always sympathetic to the vulnerable or wretched human being caught up in the turmoils of war.

He was proud of his patriotism. He was clear that he had done the right thing for his country, whether working for Collins, in the conflict of the Civil War or as head of the Garda crime branch. Yet I always felt – and it is clear from this book – that he was prone to the regrets and doubts which often afflict those who are engaged in the work of espionage. He achieved his objectives for Collins by deceiving his superiors and colleagues in the detective branch, not a few of whom were to die because they thought him one of their own. For the most part they were men like David Neligan himself, farmers' and shopkeepers' and teachers' sons from rural Ireland, caught in a conflict of duties between their nationality and their job. Neligan's own nationalism is often muted in the book and it is clear that he was torn, at times, between loyalties to his comrades in the police and his task in support of Collins's guerilla campaign.

The Spy in the Castle explores an important dimension of the Irish War of Independence and it is a significant historical document. Irish history for many years after independence shied away from the bloody reality of guerilla warfare, prefering to focus on the almost-glamorous exploits of the men of the Flying Columns or those who took part in the set-piece battles with Black and Tans or Auxiliaries. David Neligan's account tells of back-street shootings, ambushes and assassinations. When he wrote it in the late 1960s few could have anticipated that the same sordid script would shortly be played out again in Northern Ireland. *The Spy in the Castle* refers to events more than 70 years ago. But in a way, it is also a contemporary tale of Ireland.

CONOR BRADY

Conor Brady is editor of "The Irish Times". He is author of "Guardians of the Peace", (1974, Gill and Macmillan) and a number of papers on the security policy of the Irish Free State 1922-32

The author: 1923

THE SPY IN THE CASTLE

DAVID NELIGAN

Prendeville Publishing Limited

© Prendeville Publishing Limited 1999
2nd Printing December 1999

Prendeville Publishing Limited, an English company, whose
registered office is at 17 Brudenell Road, London SW17 8DB,
England.

First Published in 1968 by MacGibbon & Kee Limited, London and
printed by Ebenezer Baylis & Son Limited, The Trinity Press
Worcester and London. This edition is published by Prendeville
Publishing Ltd, London, under licence from
HarperCollins*Publishers* Ltd, London. It is a facsimile of the 1968
edition.

Prendeville Publishing Limited gratefully acknowledges the co-
operation of the National Library of Ireland in granting permission
to use a photograph from the Lawrence collection, upon which part
of the cover of this book is based.

British Library Cataloguing in Publication Data.
A Catalogue record of this book is available from the British Library

ISBN 0 9535697 0 5
Printed by ColourBooks Ltd, Dublin.

For David and Brian

FOREWORD

THIS is the story of my service with Michael Collins at the time of the Black and Tans. Everything set down is true, nothing has been exaggerated nor aught actuated by malice.

To protect innocent people, I have transposed some names and incidents without damaging the truth. Descendants of some persons mentioned live and I have no desire to embarrass them or cause pain. The story is personal and does not profess to be a history of the period.

I should like to pay a tribute to my old friend Mrs. V. Dempsey for typing the manuscript and for struggling valiantly with my awful writing: also to her colleague and my friend Miss O'Donovan and to my daughter-in-law Miriam. The Editor of the *Irish Independent*, Mr Michael Rooney, whose paper ran a series of excerpts from my story, I thank for his courtesy and kindness. A special word of thanks goes to his Assistant Editor, Mr Denis O'Connor, who presented the series with great skill and judgement and gave precious time to it. The photographic staff of the paper also deserve my sincere thanks. I am grateful to Mr Timothy O'Keeffe, Director of MacGibbon & Kee, for his kindness and encouragement. I should like to add that, like the pavement artist's, this is my own work and no literary ghost has been employed. I am very grateful to Professor J. B. Coakley, for reading the proofs.

1967   DAVID NELIGAN

ILLUSTRATIONS

I

I WAS born in Templeglantine, Co. Limerick in 1899. This place is midway between the little towns of Abbeyfeale and Newcastle West and is near the Kerry border of Co. Limerick. My parents were National School teachers, Father being a Kerryman and Mother a native of Templeglantine. I was the youngest of a family of eight, having two brothers and four sisters: another brother died in infancy. That part of Limerick is hilly and the land is not good compared with that of East and Mid-Limerick which contains some of the best land in Europe—the famed Golden Vale.

The people, most of whom were smallholders and labourers, were not badly off as they were industrious and rents were low. Mixed farming was carried on and tillage; every farmer had a few milch-cows (the Limerick red, a very fine animal, is well-known locally). A co-op. creamery takes surplus milk, makes fine butter and cheese and provides a useful cash-crop with a return to the farmer of skim-milk, useful for feeding young stock. No social divisions exist; no tuppence-ha'penny looking down on tuppence. We never had any money, but were well fed and had fun growing up.

Kevin O'Higgins used to say that anyone who had not lived in the country hadn't lived and it is true. Though rather damp at times, the climate there is very temperate, with little frost or snow and very mild winters. If it has a fault, it is that it is too moist, but even the rain has a soft caressing touch. We had a few craftsmen like carpenters and blacksmiths and a large number of farm labourers.

We lived in a portion of the old school and our quarters, like it, were in a shocking state of disrepair. No running water, rat-infested, no sewage, no lighting except paraffin-oil lamps. The school, which dated from 1829, should have been pulled down long ago. It was even badly sited, being built in a hollow. The slated roof leaked like a sieve and vicious draughts whistled through the ill-fitting windows. The sanitary arrangements, which had to cope with over two hundred pupils in summer, were of the stone-age variety. Father had to pay a man out of his own pocket to cleanse the place, or we should have had outbreaks of fever, which killed his successor. Actually this terrible disease scourged a neighbouring parish every year and took the life of the best doctor we ever had; Dr Willie McCarthy, who attended the victims with utmost devotion until he, too, succumbed. The McCarthys were Doctors for generations and were revered locally. Nothing had been spent on repairs for many a long day. It became a really vexing question.

In those times, the teachers were paid their miserable pittance quarterly and it was sent not to them but to the Parish Priest who was Manager of the school. It is scarcely credible that the British Government in Ireland (which I shall from here for convenience call the Castle) stopped the principal teachers' salaries as the school was not repaired; but such was the case. So my parents' salaries were delayed over and over again, sometimes for months on end. This was a great trial to them with a numerous young family and no other resources. It looked to them as if one day salaries would cease altogether!

Our Bishop, who lived in Limerick city, twenty-five miles away, was Dr O'Dwyer. He was friendly towards my Father who was an excellent teacher and who took great pains preparing the pupils for Confirmation, this being the only time a visitation from His Lordship took place. This question of repairing the schools went on for years. The Bishop sent us a new Parish Priest, named Fr. Breen. The school repairs were said to have an early priority. More years passed; nothing was done, and a particularly long stoppage of salary occurred. To be just, Fr. Breen offered my Father a loan but he refused it. Exasperated beyond measure at getting no salaries, he complained in writing to the Bishop who was a fierce disciplinarian and greatly feared by his clergy. He had been raised to that rank straight from a curacy. Fr. Breen and my Father had a terrible row. The school still went unrepaired. It became our King Charles' head. Discussing the matter with a local farmer, he said: 'Of course your Father was right, David, but when you have your hand in the dog's mouth . . . ' Relations between them were, to say the least, strained from that time.

A little river runs nearby and it provided us with nice brown trout. Many happy hours I squandered on its banks. In summer, the salmon trout (called locally white trout) came up from the sea and gave good sport. They are beautiful fish, with silvery sides, and an average weight of about one pound. Inside, they are of a paler pink than salmon and in my opinion of a superior flavour. Sympathy would be wasted on anyone dining on a broiled white-trout and a rasher of home-cured bacon!

In summer, my brothers and I chased about in bare feet and spent hours fishing, swimming and in the hurling field, so that we were always fit, barring accidents. Fishing, our lures were generally wet flies on a light cast or in heavy water, 'blue-head' worms and Stuart's tackle. A few miles away is the Feale, a fine salmon river, but we never bothered going farther away than a mile or two.

My Father loved reading and though far from the centre of happenings, liked to keep in touch with affairs. Every morning I had to go to a local level-crossing where a friendly guard threw out a copy of a morning paper: *The Cork Examiner*. Though, of course, a road led to that place, I used to do the two miles cross-country until I was about nine or ten, when a donkey stood on my bare foot with his iron-shod hoof and put a stop to my gallop. This caused a wound which cost me a year flat on my back. It became infected and the pain was excruciating: every night for months my poor Mother had to come to my bed to try and comfort me as I cried and groaned. And she had to teach school next day. How she must have suffered!

My Father cycled fifty miles to procure a herbal cure known as Moriarty's Plaster. It was a lovely green shade and had to be warmed before application. I cannot say it did any good. The Doctor told my Father I had T.B. and the flesh fell off my bones. Mother, a person of surpassing faith, prayed for me every day

11

and every night. The only medicament available in those days was iodoform, a compound of iodine, a weak antiseptic: to this day the smell of it nauseates me. However, thanks be to God and to Mother's prayers, the injury began to heal, closed up and left no ill-effects.

We had a good landlord, Lord Devon, whom we neither saw nor knew but felt his beneficence at long range. Like Ernie O'Malley's battalion commander, he was a semi-mythical being. Originally, he or his forebears donated seven acres of land, free of tax or rent, to the school and his agent, one Captain Curling, was ordered to pay the schoolmaster £10 a year as well. Even in the 'bad times' he never evicted anyone and his rents were always reasonable: in fact he was a paragon amongst landlords. His name is preserved locally, a road being called after him.

As my Mother taught school all day for five days a week, we had a poor woman named Bridge Connors housekeeping. She reared us, spoilt us and put up with all our tantrums. One day she missed me and my infant sister Joan. As the little river was in spate she ran to it and found us sailing down the flood in a wash-tub. Fortunately the current wafted it to the bank and she grabbed it; she boxed Joan's ears and kissed me!

When my parents were in Ballybunion she was left at home to mind us. The local lads used to play tricks to frighten her. Once at Christmas she put currant cakes on the window-sill to cool and the wren boys* took them to annoy her. They used to scare her at night too.

My Father and Mother were self-educated. There were no teachers' training colleges then. They had started teaching as monitors, a rank now largely defunct. A monitor then was a senior pupil who received an even more minute salary than later, if he decided on a life of slow starvation teaching.

Father and Mother studied all their lives and were devoted to their profession. Father taught senior pupils extra subjects such as algebra and Euclid, for which he received no payment. Mother, a native speaker of Irish, taught the language for forty years when it was not so popular or profitable as it is today.

* Boys in rural Ireland who go collecting from houses on St Stephen's day, and dance and sing.

12

We had somewhat irregular sessions of night-school for the family and this was conducted by Father, when he could corral us from the river and the hurling field. When he was in funds, which was not often, he would cycle to Abbeyfeale and have a few drinks with his cronies. Then we escaped night-school and how thankful we were. Carting the oil-lamps about was hazardous and the glass globes were forever breaking. I often wonder we did not have a fire.

At irregular intervals we were visited by school inspectors, important fellows in those days, whose reports could make or mar a teacher. They made Newcastle West their base, coming to us on an outside car. The hotelier, Mr Curtin, who was friendly to Father and Mother, sent them a warning signal in time. When the local P.O. got the phone installed he used it.

Mr Hogan, senior inspector, was examining us one day and a senior lad was reading aloud. Old Hogan corrected his pronunciation of some word which I've forgotten. Father was not having any, though, and whitefaced said: 'I beg your pardon Sir, the boy is quite right. I'll show you the dictionary!' Needless to say the class was charmed at this diversion and hoped for a stand-up fight, not caring a damn about that or any word.

To be honest, though, I must say Mr Hogan kept his temper admirably. To the lad he said, 'Go on with your reading, boy,' and to the Master, 'We will discuss this later.' I had visions of the old man being fired then and there and shamelessly eavesdropped outside the door.

Both of them had it 'hot and heavy' but not only did the Inspector not report him adversely, but gave a favourable report on the school which says something for his magnanimity.

The dictionary Father produced that day is still in my possession. It is in two volumes, one now badly dog-eared. The other he had repaired by a bookbinder page by page, but when he got the bill the other stayed dog-eared. Dictionaries have not the last word in pronunciation, which often alters in a few years.

Another day an inspector arrived on an outside car in the snow. It was about two minutes after the official closing time of 3 p.m. and he went straight to Mother's school and opened the roll-book. Before he had time to examine it (it may have been out of plumb) Father arrived at a run, snatched it away and told the official to return during official hours.

This man, Mr Morgan, was in the last stages of T.B. and it was a miracle how he kept going. He did not report the incident nor did he return, but he did warn my Father against the machinations of an enemy. Poor Mr Morgan was found drowned in the Shannon some time afterwards; peace to his ashes.

He was succeeded by Mr J. McMahon, a stout fellow with a big head, loud voice and a hearty laugh. He used to time his visits to coincide with a famous coursing meeting at Clounanna where once, he told Father, he had lost his month's salary backing dogs.

One day in school he asked us what the word 'insular' meant and nobody knew, but I thought I did and put up my hand. 'Well, boy?' 'It's the white cap on the telephone pole, Sir!' He guffawed.

The last time he came in style, in a chauffeur-driven model T Ford and gave a crowd of us a jaunt; we did not mind walking back. Years afterwards I attended the poor fellow's funeral, for old times' sake.

Some amusing characters dwelt in our parish. Jacky Alley, an old labourer, lived in an out-of-the-way, nearly uninhabited place. Someone said that to him one day and he replied: 'It's a bloody great place. You wouldn't see a priest or a policeman from one end of the year to th'other!' He was saving hay with a farmer who had a son a priest, and they had a row. Jacky said: 'Many a man in Holy Orders had a rogue of a father!' Being quick on his feet saved his hide that day.

His wife died and her remains were brought to the chapel on the shoulders of four six-footers. Jacky was a tiny fellow and was hard put to keep up with those giants. 'Aisy! Aisy! Men, for the love of God, it's no stolen goods ye have!' he cried.

When Campbell-Bannerman's government introduced old-age pensions, Jacky attended the presbytery to procure his birth certificate. Standing on the doorstep was a neighbouring farmer who was not too fond of Jacky, from whose barbed tongue he had often suffered. 'Begod, Mr Acres, I never thought I'd see the day when we'd be beggars on the same doorstep!' It is a pity

14

nobody collected his epigrams. My Father, a voracious reader, was often short of material, so I had to search the parish for the loan of a book. Later, a library was opened in Newcastle West. Once I was given *The Sayings of Poor Richard* by Ben. Franklin, the American revolutionary, and also his autobiography. They came from U.S.A.

Campbell-Bannerman's government issued a decree authorising night-schools for adults. They were to be taught (free) the three R's, and teachers' fees were fairly decent. Father said to Mother: 'I suppose no one here will attend, but I'll put up a notice anyway.'

So a notice in his beautiful script appeared on our wall-newspaper, the chapel gate, next Sunday. Classes were to commence on the following night in the month of September. Fires were lit, so were the oil-lamps, ink-bottles were filled; the assistant teachers came. Father look out of the window and cried to Mother, 'Madam! Come here!'

The yard was thronged with people. Young, old, middle-aged, they had walked miles in a deluge of rain, this being their first chance to have a little schooling. All most of them wanted was to be able to write their names, or maybe a letter to relatives in America, for there was hardly one whose kin had not emigrated there. So the classes were a resounding success.

Alas! They did not last, for some other gang of politicians got into power, and that was the end of it.

Like the story of Henry Longhurst, the famous golfing writer; between the wars he wrote a readable book about his travels and the title was *It was good while it lasted*. He became an M.P. but lost his seat in due course, and the night the votes were counted, a wag in the crowd shouted: 'It was good while it lasted, Henry!' Such men are dangerous!

Both my grandmothers were nearly ninety when they died. They remembered the Great Famine which occurred in their youth, and remembered seeing people eating nettles on the road-side. Nearby is a meadow still known as the Depot, where Indian meal (maize) was rationed to the people, unfortunately after hordes of them had died. The population of Ireland was halved in those terrible days. Four million people died or emigrated.

15

We kept two cows and tilled part of our little holding; hay had to be bought, though, for winter feeding.

A wet summer came, the meadow which Father bought was too soft for a mowing machine. So I was sent up the hill to ask Bill Regan to mow it. He was a tiny fellow with bronzed face, his lithe body beautifully muscled. He lived in a small thatched cottage with his decent wife and a numerous family, all industrious and neatly built, like him.

'Faith, David,' says he, 'I haven't an hour to spare between now and the end of harvest, but sure I'll do the Master's bit.' When he started I was sent to the meadow with tea and buttered soda-bread. He had been there since dawn. The tracks of his bare feet were ruler-straight across the sward; so were the swathes which he mowed with a beautiful economy of movement.

At intervals, he sharpened the scythe with a whetstone, finishing off with an abrasive board, until the steel was razor-sharp. He wore only trousers; his shirt was spread on a bush.

Like every lad, always asking questions, I asked him why. 'Faith, David, so that it'll be fine and dry in the evening.' He was an adept with the poor crooked scythe and spade. Mowing was one operation I could not master, either sticking the point of the scythe in the ground or nearly amputating my legs. Sharpening it was also dangerous as one could inflict a nasty injury on the hands if not deft enough. The saying about edged tools certainly has force here.

Two elderly bachelor brothers named Connors lived nearby. They were farm labourers and experts with spades. They were also a bit cracked and miserly. As honest as the day and terrific workers, they would not spend a penny on themselves nor on their miserable cabin. Every halfpenny went into the P.O. savings bank.

Father sent me to their home to ask them to sow some potatoes. Used as I was to bad housing, their domicile shocked me. The one-roomed thatched hut was even older than the school and did not contain one stick of furniture except an old iron pot and two tin mugs. They slept on boughs of trees on the mud floor, without benefit of sheets or blankets. They were of middle age, charming

16

fellows, without an ounce of flesh on them. Wherever they worked they were fed, otherwise they'd have died of malnutrition.

One, the more crack-brained of the two, was nicknamed *Ceanneen* in Gaelic, i.e. head-case, and he actually did die in the winter-time. The survivor did nothing about burying him and the Relieving Officer (a kind of Poor Law official) arranged for his funeral. Much later he called to the brother. 'I've come about your poor brother, the Lord have mercy on him, with a little account of £3 for the funeral.' 'He's dead and buried now and let him rest. There's no use in raking up them things!' The ratepayers had to pay, under some subhead.

Local lads used to listen outside the hut to the two talking: 'Of course,' said one, 'I could go to the shop for a side of bacon, but sure everything the bastard has is rotten.'

Once I was present in another shop, the P.O., when the elder came in. He started to complain about the hard times.

The Postmaster, who long ago had them sized up, presented him with a withdrawal form and a pen: 'Here,' says he, 'sign this and you can withdraw £10 for food.' He vanished without a word. Some wit has said that a miser is a curse to live with but makes a marvellous ancestor.

The parish was practically free of crime. Doors were never locked (a cynic might say we had nothing worth stealing), farm tools could be left out in fields, livestock were never stolen, the people were downright honest. Only two incidents involving violence occurred.

One night when Father was on holidays in Lisdoonvarna, a Co. Clare spa, a drunken youth called to the school. He started yelling like a Red Indian and smashed up a large barrel used for watering cows. His yells terrified Mother and the rest of us and she had the front door locked. As she said: 'he was out of his mind from drink'. He belonged to a decent but rather wild family.

Next day he appeared, with downcast mien, to apologise. 'You damned blackguard,' said Mother, 'you will go to the gallows yet!'

The Great War broke out and he disappeared. Said to have joined the British Navy, he made no signal for a long time. So his poor old mother called to ask Father to enquire. He used to act as letter-writer for many people, even petitioning the Lord Lieutenant on one occasion, on behalf of some poor devil in prison.

He wrote to the Secretary of the Admiralty as to the whereabouts of the son. He sent me to her home with the reply which I read to the poor woman: it was from Whitehall.

'I am directed by the Lords Commissioners of the Admiralty to refer to your letter of . . . relative to the location of Stoker Hulton. I am to express the regret of my Lords that consequent on injuries received in an affray at Gibraltar this man died on such a date.' A money order was enclosed.

While I read in that poor room, tears coursed down the old mother's cheeks. My heart went out to her. She remembered him only as a toddler lisping his first words. With a heavy heart, I left her the letter and enclosure and went away in silence.

The other incident concerned a poor man who took up a job carting cream and butter from the creamery to the railway station. He was known as 'T'honleen', i.e. the only one. The snag was that his predecessor had gone on strike for higher wages and was sacked.

Armed men broke into T'honleen's house one night and gave him a terrible beating. Though frail of body and tiny, he recovered and went on with the job, bloody but unbowed. He received protection from two armed Royal Irish Constabulary men who lived in his house and accompanied him everywhere.

A new head constable arrived at their station. He was a strict disciplinarian. Thinking those two were having it too soft, he arrived one scorching day and drilled them up and down the road until they were ready to drop.

Cycling by after this exercise, I saw both of them lying under a tree in an exhausted condition. They woke up, though, sufficiently to commission me to bring them a half-gallon of stout from Abbeyfeale and gave me an earthenware jar. As this is a very awkward object on a bicycle, I cursed the two of them heartily. They were still in that post years afterwards when I left the place.

The Dublin morning papers now circulated in the locality and I had to cycle to the railway station a couple of miles away for ours.

18

The station master was Ben Lenihan, a Corkman. A stoutly built man with a red face, he was an enterprising fellow. To eke out his poor wages, he used to rent land from neighbouring farmers who were too lazy to work it.

On these fields he reared Kerry ponies, lovely little spirited grey-coloured animals, and a herd of miniature Kerry cows, all blacks with shining coats and silver horns. Often I stood at the field gate with Ben.

He would whistle and the ponies came flying. He generally had a lump of sugar or some other titbit for them.

The little cows gave a fine milk-yield and it was said that it contained no T.B. germs. Certainly, if fresh air could combat that fell disease, the germs would not stand a dog's chance on top of the mountains where those little animals were reared.

Ben had a marvellous way with animals and taught us how one could live comfortably with the aid of enterprise and industry; a useful lesson, if we'd only profited by it.

He was a stickler for punctuality, and if a farmer arrived for a load of lime five minutes after closing time, he found the gate firmly locked. Years afterwards when he was in the upper eighties, he came to see me, down-to-earth as ever and still working, making mattresses he told me. Here was one industrious Irishman!

Turf (peat) was our fuel for heating and cooking. The neighbouring townland of Sugarhill contained vast bogs and one could hire a 'bank' for a few shillings. This would yield a year's supply. The turf was cut by hand; this was completely a manual task.

My brothers and I used to go with the men, in May, to the bog. A convoy of asses and carts left in the dawn (the ground was too soft after winter rain, for horses) and every party brought rations, consisting of soda-bread, fresh butter, home-cured bacon and tea. These expeditions were great fun and those men were cheerful and amiable companions.

The bog, a great plain, stretched for miles and was now covered with a carpet of young heath, asphodel and bog-cotton. The sky was filled with the song of larks, and occasionally a brood of grouse flew by with a frightened cry. Their solitude had been disturbed for the first time that year.

The first operation was to strip the bog. This was done with the aid of a hay-knife which cut the grass into strips.

A garden spade was used to clean off the top sod which, consisting of heather and tough grass, was useless for firing but filled holes in the spreading-ground.

The turf-cutter, armed with an L-shaped spade, called a sléan, then started cutting each sod. This was deftly caught by a helper with a hay-fork and slung up to another who carted the sods to the drying ground in a barrow. There it was spread out by others to dry in the wind and sun.

Then it was turned to be dried on the other side and later raised into little heaps. This was known as 'footing', was generally done by women and was a back-breaking job.

When the turf was dried, each sod was reduced to half its original size and if of good black quality, was nearly as good a fuel as coal.

The final process was to clamp it in a rick near the road where it could be drawn home by a horse cart and creel.

In fine weather the sun and wind did the job without much trouble, but when the summer came wet, it was a form of slavery as no crop is so much at the mercy of the weather. I am told that labour is now so scarce and dear that turf-cutting is largely a thing of the past, which is to be regretted.

At midday, someone was sent to make a fire and get water boiled for tea. All over the bog, one could see dozens of turf fires with smoke ascending like a prayer. Nowhere does tea taste better. I never knew of anyone to complain of loss of appetite there and we used to eat like horses. The hard work in the keen champagne-like air made us ravenous. All the farmers sent horses to draw home the Master's turf. A barrel of stout was available for them that day!

When the British Government granted labourers a half-acre site for a cottage, a local man chose a very wet plot in the bog for his home. Seeing him fencing it, a passer-by said: 'Why did you pick such a wet oul' place, Mick?' The man stuck his spade in the slush and leant on it. He pointed to a lark in the heavens. 'Do you see that lad up there? He could be below in the demesne if he like!' Jacky Alley was not the only wit we had.

A farmer going home from town with an empty creel was accosted by an inquisitive neighbour. 'You were at the market, Dan?' 'I was.' 'Did you bring in the pig?' 'I did.' 'I see you sold her?' 'I did.' 'Did you get a good price?' 'I did, but I didn't do as well as I expected, but then I didn't expect that I would.'

All our farmers and some labourers reared pigs. If they did not keep sows they bought piglets and fattened them with skim milk, potatoes, maize meal and farm refuse. The best of this diet was Indian (corn) or maize meal. It came from U.S.A. and was very cheap then—about 5s. per cwt. Of reddish yellow colour, it was ground very small and a fist-full in white flour made a palatable cake. Some frugal people made both cakes and porridge out of it; nothing so cheap or good could be grown here, unfortunately. Cottoncake was good fattening food but too dear.

At Christmas, most people had a fat pig to kill and make bacon. A pig of about twelve stones was thought to be best, anything heavier would be too fat. Farmers sometimes killed enormous old sows, though.

Mike Roche, an amateur butcher, came to kill our pig. That was the day! An amiable giant, he was an expert, and as clean as a new pin. With a large, sharp-pointed knife he stuck the pig through the heart in one second. A road-worker, he gave his services free to his friends. Tubs of boiling water were at hand, and helpers shaved the pig with sharp knives. The carcass was hung up, disembowelled and left for a day or two. Then it was cut up and salted.

Salting was a laborious job and the salt rubbed in well with the aid of little brushes worn on the hands. This went on for several hours, then the pieces were packed in a barrel with layers of salt. After some days, brine was poured in and left until the meat was cured which took a matter of some weeks. It was taken out and hung up on the kitchen ceiling. Properly done, home-cured bacon is good eating, but not for everybody on account of the salt. Still, for those following arduous labour in the open air, it was nourishing food. I've seen farmers eating it three times a day, six days a week, and they thrived on it!

The woman of the house and her helpers made puddings. Into these went the blood, onions, and various 'spare parts' of the pig.

A good housewife made excellent puddings and gave them as presents to friends. If well made, they are very well worth eating.

Lent was strictly kept in those days—black tea, dry bread and an austere fast. Every farmer kept a barrel of salted herrings and some a large fish called ling, of the cod family. This too was salted and tasted like leather. After half a century the mere thought of it fills me with loathing, as the Yank said of the bully beef.

One year turf was scarce owing to a bad spring and a man bought a rick. When he came to bring it home, he found the rascal had built the rick around a huge rock. He did nothing about it. It was unheard of to go to law or to call the police. A fellow who stooped to those sharp tricks was very unpopular and was shunned.

Father bought a cow once, and she had no teeth! The first thing a farmer does is to look into the animal's mouth, but the Schoolmaster was too polite as he knew the vendor. Nemesis overtook the latter, but as details would serve to identify him, I'll say no more.

Often I was sent to Listowel for a leg of mutton. The train brought me and the fare was twopence return for a round journey of about fifteen miles, and the railways made a profit then!

Dan Flavin, a friend of Father's, kept a neat bookshop there and presented me with a copy of *The Three Musketeers*. He was a friend of everyone who loved books, and gave away hundreds. A broad-shouldered man with bristly hair and an artificial leg, the last time I saw him he was a political prisoner. That was in 1923.

2

DAN REEVES was the only delinquent we had. He was a petty thief. A sturdily built man of middle age, a squint gave him a sinister look. He had a lisp and a sense of humour, somewhat twisted, like his eye. No one knew his origin, and he had no home.

If driven to it, he did an odd day's labouring with a farmer, but that was rare. He had a weakness for poultry diet and often raided fowl-houses. Having acquired a fat bird, he retired to a hilly field which had a deposit of malleable clay. He worked this up and wrapped the fowl in it, without benefit of plucking or cleaning. He then made a fire of bracken and faggots, thrusting the ball of clay into the centre when it reached oven temperature. When the fire died down, he cracked open the ball and had roast fowl and no trace of a feather. Local people supplied him with bread and tea.

Sometimes, in a puckish spirit, he stole things of no earthly use to him, e.g. one hundred jute sacks from a farmer who expected the threshers. If the farmer had caught Dan that day, more than the oats would have had a threshing. The police always kept on his tracks, and many a trip he made to Tralee jail; in fact he made a ballad about it, 'Tralee jail would kill the devil'.

Our nearest police station was in the hamlet of Tournafulla, manned by a sergeant and four or five constables of the Royal Irish Constabulary. It was a semi-military force and everything about it had to be shipshape, including the garden plot. The R.I.C. used to round up Dan every spring and make him till this plot free. The potato drills had to be ruler-straight, like Bill Regan's swathes.

One day, the station party had to attend court and left Dan to till the plot. When they returned, the drills presented the appearance of a crazy pavement, meandering in every direction. The horrified Sergeant tackled Dan. 'Why in hell didn't you straighten the drills?' 'How the blazes could I, when the bloody wope was cwooked?' They troubled him no more.

Meeting him once on the road, he asked me to bring him fourpence-worth of Epsom salts from the local shop. He got two large packets, perhaps two or three ounces. Taking an old tin from the ditch, he rinsed it at the pump, threw in all the salts, stirred it with a stick, poured in a little water and swallowed the lot, while I looked on wide-eyed. Years later he was run down by a car and died of his injuries.

Every summer a festival was held in the town of Killorglin, Co. Kerry, known as Puck Fair. This saturnalia is said to have had its origins in pagan times, which I can well believe. It was a Mecca for all the tinkers and travelling people within a fifty-mile radius. For a week before the fair, convoys of them with asses, horses, caravans and cur-dogs passed our house at all hours. No farmer with lands bordering the roads got any sleep that week, having to watch his crops from those nomads who had numerous live-stock and no feed bills.

Once a tinker passing by had a row with his woman and struck her with an iron chain off the cart. Her screams brought men running from a hayfield, and they gave him a few wallops. The women tinkers were just as tough as their men.

The people were very generous to tinkers, never refusing them a little flour, potatoes, meal or milk for the children. Nobody ever asked them to do any work; it was well understood that they were allergic to it. Rabbits were plentiful then, and a useful part of their diet, they being skilled trappers. Sometimes they fished the rivers, and slept under dry arches of a bridge. Sudden rainstorms sometimes drowned the poor wretches in those places. Now, their hazard is traffic.

A tinker met a man who carried a large pike. 'That's a small fish, Sir.' 'What do you call a large one?' 'One about a foot.' 'Blast you, this one is three feet.' 'Ah, yes, Sir, but we measure them between the eyes!'

Our labouring men used to hire out to farmers in the rich low-lands in East Limerick. The term was for eleven months and the wages, living in, about £12. Farm work in those days was back-breaking toil. Most of those men emigrated to U.S.A. after a few years of it. We were about the only family in the parish who did not receive money from America at Christmas. Perhaps they thought we were too rich!

A neighbour went to America before the First War and returned in the uniform of an army sergeant. Outside the chapel gate on Sunday he was greeted by all, including his old employer, Marty Spartan. 'How do you like the Army, Jack?' He hitched up his belt and straightened his back. 'Begod, boys, it's not so bad; you'd be a long time working for Marty there before he'd tell you stand at ease!' Even Marty laughed at this sally.

The new labourers' cottages were not a bad job, when the contractor was honest and competent (too often he wasn't), and a great improvement on the thatched cabins with mud floors. I have seen whole families in those hovels wiped out by T.B. which then was, like drink, a national scourge. Windows were always too small and not made to open. The germs, it may be supposed, had a happy medium in the mud floors and walls and in the age-old roofs. Worst off of all was a family breathing infected air and the contagion from sputum. Often it could be seen that the men of a family escaped while the womenfolk were wiped out. One old man smoked thatch as he could not afford tobacco, and he lived to be ninety!

The rent of a cottage was very low, generally a shilling a week, so that they were a Godsend to those poor people. It cannot be said though that a farm labourer's life is anything but arduous and badly paid. It is hard to see how the average farmer can afford to pay better. It is really a vexing question, which has not yet been solved, if it is capable of solution. 'Small' farmers are just as badly off.

Oul' Connors was over seventy years old, but a man of powerful physique. He was one of those lucky people who got by with little effort and yet was not badly off. He was great fun and had strong views on matters in general.

Wounds on man or beast were best treated with a liberal

25

application of cart-grease which came in a flat tin and cost about sixpence per pound. As it had been boiled in manufacture and grew mouldy in time if left open to the air, Connors could be said to have discovered penicillin instead of Fleming! Joking aside, though, it was strange that injuries so treated did not go septic. To the day of his death at the age of eighty, from a respiratory disease, he swore by cart-grease.

His Uncle Mick was the hero of all his stories. Whether Mick had any corporeal existence I never knew. Mick had a marvellous greyhound which could run like the wind, until one day it broke its leg in a rabbit-burrow. A listener asked: 'Did he have to put him down?' 'Not at all. Uncle Mick cut down his other legs and made a wonderful terrier out of him.'

Mick was a smashing footballer. His opponent in a match had protruding teeth. The pitch was lined with immemorial elms. Mick and Toothy were running hell-for-leather for the ball. Mick gave him a terrific 'choulder' which put him flying into a tree; 'not a dentist in Ireland could have made a better job of him'.

My Father loved listening to Connors, who could keep up these tales for hours, aided by a few bowls of stout. To get his own back on Connors, Father told him a few yarns from *The Fabulous Adventures of Baron Münchausen*, the work of a German called Raspe who was said to have lived or died at Killarney. Later, at a wake, Father heard Oul' Connors telling one or two of those as having happened to Uncle Mick and improving on Münchausen.

Mick Lacey, the blacksmith, came out of his forge one day as a funeral passed by. Behind the cortège walked Paty Susy, a man of the roads. He was about four feet in height and weighed about three stone, his face had an unearthly pallor; anyone seeing him for the first time could not imagine that he'd live another day. 'Damn me!' said Lacey, 'that's a strange funeral, with the corpse walking behind!' Lacey's neighbour had some hilly land stocked with dry cattle; he also had a dog, Jaguar, which he could be heard calling half the day. Jaguar disappeared one day and the owner asked Lacey had he seen it. 'Yes.' 'Where?' 'Going down to the river to drown itself.'

I often watched the sparks fly in the forge; Lacey and his aged

26

father had wonderful hands and could make or mend anything made of iron. Alas, the terrible 'flu of 1918 killed him, but Paty Susy survived.

We had a junior hurling team which never made headlines but was good fun. Hurleys are a sort of wide hockey sticks and those sold in shops then were limbs of ash trees and too brittle.

The best hurleys are made from the roots of an ash tree with the grain running true along the boss. To procure those of course, a tree with suitable roots is required; these are scarce. One can see whether the tree is likely to yield good hurleys and we inspected many. The tree of course has to be uprooted, a hefty job.

Eventually we located a beauty on a hillside farm. So Tadg Horan the Captain and elderly fans approached the owner one Sunday and asked him for the tree. He refused. His grandfather, God be good to him, had planted that tree and he might turn in his grave if he saw it being dug up. Farmers are conservative people.

The boys thanked him for his homily. A council of war was held. It was decided unanimously that the tree should be dug up without delay. About twenty of us attacked it one moonlit night with pickaxes, hatchets and crowbars.

First we cut the trunk about three feet from the ground and dug up the stump, finishing off by putting the trunk back in the hole. We borrowed a farmer's cart (when he wasn't looking) on which we wheeled the stump to the nearby railway line where the Captain, a plate-layer, had a bogey waiting. The son of the cart-owner told us afterwards that the weight had strained the axle of the cart; he could not keep it out of the ditch.

With much heaving and grunting, we got our stump on the bogey trundling it to a railway station, whence it was conveyed to a sawmill by train next day—no freight payable.

For a few shillings, the sawmill people rough-cut the hurleys, a hurler on the staff giving expert advice. We fined down those shapes with planes, spokeshaves and sandpaper until we were satisfied with the result. Frequently we oiled the hurleys to keep the ash supple and sweet. The grain was beautiful.

Shop-made hurling-balls then were covered with sheep or horse-skin which, too light when dry, became sodden when wet and lost all bounce, in fact became lethal weapons. Some wise man suggested to us that ass's skin might be better and tougher. We decided to experiment. We'd try anything once, especially if it cost nothing. A man nearby had an old donkey with a bad leg; it should have been destroyed years before. Borrowing Father's old single-barrel, my brothers and I with some neighbouring lads marched the ass to a river bank where it was shot.

As soon as he had fallen, lads with sharp knives flayed him. Others dug the grave. Years afterwards the Black and Tans dug it up! Selected portions of the skin were scraped clean, the hair burned off with lime. It was then buried in the bog, which helped to tan it. In due course we had nearly black leather, of good quality, wonderfully supple, tough and waterproof.

We then fashioned a cork core and wound yards of Mother's woollen thread tightly round it. An old shop ball opened up provided a pattern for the cover (two figures of eight) which was sewn with waxed hempen thread and an awl. This ball was a great success and our pride and joy.

Visiting the sawmill, my brother Maurice told us they ran films there at night, so a crowd of us cycled ten miles in the snow to our first (and last) film show in the town. Everybody on the screen seemed to be running and it was so jerky we got headaches.

Bill Rooney was our goalkeeper. An ageing labourer and a bachelor, his only love was hurling. One day he arrived to work with a spade on one shoulder and a hurley on the other and so late that his boss enquired whether it was breakfast or dinner he'd like.

Annually, in the spring, a selection committee picked the team, after Mass, outside the church. Each man was called out of the crowd. Bill was standing there waiting the call. He was ignored. I was called in his place. White-faced, he left, never speaking to one of us again. Being jilted by a woman is bad enough, but being discarded by a hurling team must be the end! At the time I thought it silly of him, but now can sympathise with the poor devil.

When we played away from home it was an occasion. The team travelled in a brake (locally: longcar) drawn by Bill Mack's team

28

of spanking blacks. Bill kept them going full pelt. The brake had primitive springs and brakes, and iron-shod wheels which hopped off the awful patches of flint on the road with bone-shattering effect, but what did we care? The roads were very bad in those days, consisting of masses of flinty stones which were simply shovelled on and left for traffic to grind down. In wet weather, the road turned to a sea of mud; in dry, one could trace a car for miles by the clouds of dust, so that it was hard to know which was worse.

Bicycle tyres made a bad battle with the razor-sharp flints. Punctures were plentiful. No one locally owned a motor-car, but as our road was the main line to Killarney, we saw plenty of English tourists. The roads also had wicked bends and hump-backed bridges, but of course motor traffic then was slow and negligible, and all other merely animal traction.

Jimeen Fitz was an itinerant stone-mason, who acted as our goalkeeper. He settled down in our parish, going from one house, to another. A farmer showed him a wall he had built. Jimeen looked at it with all the contempt a pro. reserves for an amateur, and commented: 'It's only the Will of God keeps it standing.'

My brother Maurice and sister Bridget passed the King's Scholarship examination and went away to teachers' training colleges. Brother Sean went to Cork to train as a Marconi operator; Mary Margaret went to a boarding school. I felt lonely for all of them. Having left school, I started to till our fields. We grew all sorts of vegetables, peas, beans, cauliflower, Brussels sprouts, beetroot, carrots and parsnips. We had plenty of flowers also. All tillage had to be done the hard way, with a spade. Owing to the Great War, labour was not available, and there was no money to pay for it.

I joined the local Volunteers. A split had occurred (following the usual Irish pattern), Redmond had half of them and Sinn Fein the rest. To this day I do not know which faction we supported.

The Captain decided on a day's outing to Ballybunion, a pleasant resort on the Atlantic coast of Kerry. It was the 15th August, 1917, a feast day when the place was packed with holiday-makers. We travelled by train to Listowel within eight miles of the place. Then we entrained on the Lartigue railway. It was an extraordinary contraption—a monorail invented by a Frenchman who gave his name to it. It had small twin engines, side by side, and ran on one tripod rail raised about two feet off the ground. As it was parted down the middle like a pair of panniers, everything in the way of freight had to be evenly balanced. The apparatus moved at a steady clip of about 20 m.p.h. which was quite enough in those times. This was my first and last trip on it as it folded shortly afterwards and fell into ruin.

We had no arms except wooden guns, and no equipment save haversacks and uniform hats. Forming up at the station, we marched down the main street led by the Captain. In the middle of the town, where we were the target of all eyes, he turned to us with a wide smile. 'Boys! I think we'll halt!' he said, and fell flat on his face in the dust. His haversack disgorged an empty whiskey bottle.

The war raged. Father used to read the papers aloud for the neighbours. It was the time of those awful battles of the Somme when thousands of British soldiers were mown down in Haig's 'Offensives'. The people were horrified at the carnage. A farmer who owned dry cattle sat on a table listening and bored. 'God blast them!' he cried. 'Is there anything in it about the foot and mouth?'

The British threatened to enforce conscription in Ireland, as cannon fodder was getting scarce. Posters appeared on dead walls showing St. Patrick appearing to Pat the ploughman, entreating him to go fight for little Belgium, now ground under the tyrant's heel. Plenty joined up, too, and lived to regret it. It was true—what the poet said about the Irish—they fought every nation's battles but their own.

Father was ageing and near pension-time; there was no future in the place for me. I decided to clear out.

Above: the figure
of Justice over the
upper gate,
Dublin Castle;
the Castle skyline.

Right:
Lord French and
the man who tried
to kill him on 19th
December, 1919,
M.Savage.

Above: Seamus Robinson, Sean Treacy, Dan Breen and Michael Brennan.
Below: MacDonnell, Kehoe, Slattery (from left, seated); Byrne and Daly,
Members of the squad.

3

AT THIS TIME and until the end of the British regime there were two police forces in Ireland. The Royal Irish Constabulary policed the country outside Dublin. This city was policed by the Dublin Metropolitan Police. These forces were familiarly known by their initials, R.I.C. and D.M.P.

The R.I.C. was a semi-military force armed with short carbines, a kind of light rifle, and ·45 revolvers, and was organised somewhat on army lines. At the same time to describe it as a fighting force would be wrong. It had neither the strength nor armament for anything bigger than a village riot.

Both forces had been created by Sir Robert Peel in 1836, hence the name Peelers and Bobbies. The R.I.C. strength was approximately 10,000, that of the D.M.P. 1,200.

The R.I.C. stations dotted the countryside, held three or four men, and were generally strategically placed at cross-roads. Very little escaped their notice. Recruits came from the small-farming class and had to have a smattering of education and good physique. It attracted a good type of man in peace-time and they married in their own class. No odium attached to them at this time. It was just a job. Their children got good education, and at one time ran the Civil Service, religious orders, and many other professions.

Promotion in both forces was as a result of examinations and open to Irish Roman Catholics. This was the case, though, only so far as junior ranks were concerned. The top brass was reserved for English or Irish Protestants and Freemasons. For let there be no mistake, religious and racial discrimination was rife in Government circles in Ireland. Germany was not the only place where the Herrenvolk idea flourished.

Several men from our parish were in the police, most in the D.M.P. They were all ex-pupils of our school, and quiet, decent fellows. At this time the R.I.C. was popular enough, though later, as will be seen, the opposite was true. I asked a few of them on holidays what the life was like and got glowing accounts.

It appeared that it was money for jam: the duty was so easy that one got paid for strolling around. Those fellows cut a dash when on leave; they wore fine suits, good hats and shoes and cycled about on bicycles with strengthened frames. Money jingled in their pockets.

D.M.P. men I consulted advised me to join that force. The R.I.C. was no good and you were stuck for years at some cross-road, they said. Having seen enough of cross-roads, I thought that the argument had some force, so decided to apply for the D.M.P.

I wrote to the Commissioner at Dublin Castle in January 1918, without consulting any of the family. Back came some forms which Father simply burned—he neither wanted me to join nor to go away. Determined now, I wrote again, giving the address of a friend, who also applied. A second reply came in a few days. We were directed to go to the nearest police station in the village of Tournafulla. There we were received in kindly manner by Sergeant Power, who gave us tea.

The little station shone with care, cleanliness and whitewash; four carbines cleaned and oiled hung on racks on the wall. The Sergeant, a well-set-up man of about twenty-eight, was in a rather drab bottle-green uniform, tight-fitting and smart. The insignia on the stand-up collar was a crowned harp on a scarlet background.

He took our measure, in every sense of the word. He tried to get us to join the R.I.C., praising the life of a country policeman, but we refused. I wanted to go to the city, which was an unknown entity to me. I had never been in any town bigger than Limerick, our county capital. Somewhere, I'd find the streets that were paved with gold.

Some forms were filled up and I got a glowing testimonial from our P.P. Reading it, I hardly recognised myself. The next step, after some delay, was to report to the Head Constable in Abbeyfeale. This was a bigger station (the population of a place and the amount of crime governed the size of the police party) with a head, several sergeants and about seven constables.

A head constable was a senior warrant-officer and a key man. This one was named Walsh, a kindly old man, soon to retire, and a friend of my Father's. He escaped the storm which followed. He got me to write some dictation and to do a few sums in arithmetic. Getting the wrong answer in a long-division sum, he made me do it again and gave me a lecture, too!

My neighbour, who had accompanied me, was rejected for some trivial physical reason, perhaps hammer-toes. They paid more attention to one's feet than to the other end!

In April 1918 I was called to Dublin, and bade my family and cousins a tearful farewell. A day-long journey brought me to Dublin's Kingsbridge Station. There Charley Kenny, a friend of my Father's, met me and brought me to his house where he put me up. It was a clearing-house for people from our area, and Kenny and his pleasant wife were the soul of hospitality. He played the bagpipes for me; Chesterton's description hit the nail on the head: magnificent noise.

Next morning I set out for Dublin Castle, in the city centre. About twenty other recruits turned up. We were weighed and measured by a huge constable, weight-thrower Ryan from Limerick who, with his giant frame, had the face of a mediaeval saint. Old bearded Dr Oulton examined each of us, paying special attention to lungs and feet. Fallen arches could reject one—though a few years' service, heavy boots and uniform, much standing, would cause them anyway. Assistant Commissioner F. Quinn, a grave, handsome man who had risen from the ranks (a sort of miracle for a ranking R.C.) swore us in to keep the peace. He had received his promotion from a Jewish Under Secretary at the Castle, Sir Matthew Nathan.

We were marched to Kevin Street by a senior man. Our way led through mean back-streets, flanked by old tenements and tumbledown hucksters' shops. The Depot was not much better. Situated in a slum area, everything about it was ancient, dingy and shabby. The lighting arrangements were flaring jets of gas with no mantle or covering, decidedly primitive affairs. Kevin

SC–B

Street Police Station was in the same yard also a detachment of mounted police. The only redeeming feature was the aroma of roasting chocolate from a biscuit factory. But this was countered by the stench from a knacker's yard.

The Depot was staffed by Inspector Carey, Sergeant Hurley and Constable Birmingham. Carey was about fifty, a handsome man with the shape of an athlete. In his youth, he had been a famous long-distance runner and shot-putter, and his house was full of trophies. He prided himself on his physical fitness; in fact it was a fetish with him. Not a day passed that he did not putt the shot for an hour or two. A bachelor, he had no truck with the fair sex, but led a celibate life. He loved a few drinks and to put a few shillings on a racehorse. A strict disciplinarian, he could be ruthless if put to it; on the whole he was a straight man.

Hurley was about fifty also, a burly giant with protruding eyes. Sometimes they seemed to pop out of his head in anger, for he had a low boiling-point. Like most quick to anger, though, he soon forgot it and did not harbour a grudge. A simple fellow, he worked hard at his job and was a good drill instructor. Now too fat, with an alderman's waistline, he had been a member of the police tug-o'-war team. This consisted of giants. When they pulled a similar team from Guinness's Brewery, it was a festival of grunting and groaning, but the war put an end to the police sports, an annual event. Carey and Hurley were Limerick men.

Constable Birmingham, a morose giant from Co. Clare, was also a weight-thrower and a bachelor. A silent fellow, he kept his conversation at a minimum. He slept in the place and was supposed to keep an eye on us at night. Occasionally he came upstairs to our big dormitory and opened the door quietly. Old boots with iron-shod soles and vessels of dubious content rained on his head, having been suspended over the door. Though he must have been furious, he was decent enough never to report us.

Our day started at 7.30 a.m. when we were roused by a policeman from the gate. We washed and shaved. An hour's study of the Police Manual followed. Our classroom was a dusty old bandroom and Hurley took the class. Breakfast followed and consisted of bread, butter and tea. This was provided by the Crown. If one wanted extras one could have them by paying. They would be cooked by the women in the kitchen, where there was a large coal-range. The evening meal was a replica of breakfast and nobody bothered with extras, so far as could be seen. Lunch was at 1.30 p.m. The food was simple and well cooked. Often we had boiled mutton with Scotch broth and potatoes in their jackets or maybe cabbage and bacon and potatoes—never any sweet or dessert, which we did not miss. Carey planned the simple menus: not bad for a bachelor!

After breakfast each man made his bed. This was an iron frame with a hard mattress and army blankets. It had to be made in a certain manner and if not, Hurley would order it re-made.

The messroom, a large stone-floored affair, had to be mopped out daily by the recruits, using black soap and long-handled mops. I forget who cleaned the bare wooden floor of our dormitory, but it is certain that it was always spotless.

A senior squad was in the Depot, and we were not allowed to forget that we were rookies. On my first morning at breakfast, one of those seniors flung a hard half-loaf which caught me squarely in the face. Being lonely and depressed, I did not see the fun in this, but did see who flung it. Rising from my seat, I went across the room and hit him hard, blacking his eye. Hurley was not the only one with a low boiling-point! Later, on the drill-square, Hurley asked him what happened. 'Fell in the ball-alley, Sir.' 'You blackguard! Someone gave you what you richly deserved.' He was an ex-horse-boy from the Curragh and we became friends afterwards. Curiously enough, I neither heard from him nor saw him again after he left Kevin Street, in a few months.

Our day was filled with drilling on the barrack-square, learning police-duties, use of the phone, first-aid and carrying out physical drill in the gym. In wet weather we used the riding-school which had turf on the floor and was used for exercising the police horses. Those were groomed for hours every day by their riders until their coats shone; even their hoofs were blacked and polished. The troopers were immensely tall, skinny fellows and had great pride in their appearance and in their mounts. So far as could be seen, the only duty they did was to bring some official letters to the castle occasionally. Never did I see them used to control crowds or for ceremonial. Afterwards, in a new regime, they were disbanded as a waste of money, which they were, though picturesque.

The Police Manual was our Bible and had to be studied daily. It was a practical guide to police duties and gave a fair idea of how they should be performed, though the English was archaic, but who am I to complain?

In one of the first pages we were informed that membership of any secret society was forbidden, excepting the society of Freemasons. John Redmond's party had raised this in the House of Commons and were assured that it would be deleted, but there it was.

A couple of days after I left home, someone told me to fill a bucket with water out in the yard to mop the floor. The postman arrived and gave me a letter from my sister, Joan. It told how much they missed me; how lonely they were. The water overflowed and so did my tears. Carey came around the corner: 'What's wrong, boy?' 'It's my first time away from home, Sir: this is a letter,' I blubbered. He put his hand on my shoulder: 'Now, don't be upset! We all felt like that at first. You'll be all right here.' After nearly half a century I still think of those few kind words to someone friendless and lonely.

Every Saturday we had a half-day off. Carey directed me to go to his house in Kimmage to cut grass and do a little gardening. Afterwards we had tea together. It was only a small patch but nicely kept. Another policeman named Jim Eager used to be there also: he was a handy fellow. One day, after I had hoed the flower patch and gone away, Carey said to Eager that a certain shrub looked wilted and needed watering. This particular plant was the apple of his eye. It was wilted right enough, for I had cut the root unwittingly; that is Eager's story, anyway, and he's sticking to it! When my wife heard this, with wifely candour she remarked: 'Yes and you do the same today.'

Sometimes we drilled with old Lee-Enfield rifles, but we never fired them as we had no ammunition. We also fired a course with ·32 auto pistols. As we banged bullets into bags of sawdust once, Colonel Edgeworth Johnstone, the Commissioner, came to visit. He was a portly man, well set-up, about fifty. He was said to have been a champion swordsman in the British Army. It was told that he had cut a dead sheep in half with one swipe but that may have been à la Münchausen, or maybe his uncle did it.

He asked Carey: 'Would those lads fire at Sinn Feiners, Inspector?' 'Certainly, Sir,' he replied with tongue in cheek. This was eye-wash as Carey never inculcated such thoughts in our minds, contenting himself with sticking to his training last.

He had attended a drill-course with the English Brigade of Guards and when on a big parade, he would roar like a bull. Hurley, also, could be heard a long way off, when drilling. All the drill strove to strengthen our backs and legs and made us very fit, though it was a frightful bore at times.

An honorary corporal was chosen out of each squad and his duties included ordering groceries, potatoes and vegetables. He also rationed the butter at meals. I had this thankless job while in the Depot.

Across the yard was A Division Station. The D.M.P. area was divided into A, B, C, D, E and F Divisions, G Division being the detective unit. Hence the expression 'G-men'—in existence here long before their publicised American namesakes. A, B, C and D were in the city. E and F in the suburbs.

Each station had a wet canteen which sold draught stout which came in barrels direct from the brewery. It was run by a messman elected annually by all the men in the station. As well as dishing out liquor he ordered meat and vegetables for lunch each day and carved the meat. From the profits on alcohol with (it was said) a rake-off from traders, this, to the right type of man, was a lucrative job and much sought after. Canvassing was rife near election time. The south of Ireland men combined against all the others, in a good-natured manner, of course. During his term of office, a messman was excused from duty, another boon for him, and he could sleep o' nights.

Recruits were barred from the canteen, though plenty of them sneaked in when no one was looking. On Saturday nights, some turned in to the Depot far from sober, but nobody peached on them. One wild man from Wicklow had to be forcibly prevented from singing in a loud untuneful voice, regularly, on Saturday nights. He was no McCormack!

We were paid about £3 per week, and as messing was free, were well-off enough. In summer, Carey and Hurley used to have daily a half-gallon of stout from the canteen, but never drank to excess. Carey had another love also; backing horses, which showed no profit either. Hurley lived very quietly with his nice wife and only son.

When I left home, Father wrote to two brothers in the D.M.P. to keep an eye on me. They were neighbours of giant stature, bachelors and decent fellows—Puritans in fact! They used to call for me regularly and bring me for walks off out in the country. The hair-raising stories they told me about night-life in the City frightened me so much, that for several years I was afraid even to look at a woman! All the same, I owe them a debt of gratitude. Our instructors carefully avoided such topics, which now I think was a mistake. They gave us good example, though.

The Superintendent of A Division, Reilly, lived at the gate He was an old man with stiff back and a red foxy face. All the police were afraid of him. He was said to be a dangerous devil. One day I saw him in the yard in earnest conversation with an elderly station sergeant. (Roughly, this rank was similar to head constable in the R.I.C.) They looked at me as I passed.

Next day the Inspector told me to report to the Superintendent. 'Do you know where Irishtown Station is, boy?' 'No, Sir.' 'Well, you take No. 3 tram from O'Connell Bridge and you'll get there. Report to the Station Sergeant at 10 p.m. tonight.' 'Yes, Sir.'

When I did so, the man whom I'd seen in Kevin Street was on duty. 'The jailer (an old constable) will show you to your room, boy, and will call you at 7 a.m.' He did, on the dot. After shaving and breakfast, I reported to the S.S. To my surprise he directed me to search a house in the neighbourhood but did not tell me what to look for, nor did I ask him.

Rapping at the door of the place, an elderly man answered. I think his name was O'Connor. Feeling an absolute fool, I told him 'they' had sent me to search. Poking about for a few minutes and finding nothing, I cleared off.

For a long time this performance puzzled me. Recruits were never sent on such missions. I imagine this is the explanation: a vacancy existed for Chief Superintendent in the castle. This would be a big step-up for foxy-face, who was in the running. God alone, and the Commissioner know what lies he put on paper about this raid which was to impress that official with his zeal. The Station Sergeant was his toady and they picked a recruit so that no one would know who was behind it. Anyway he got the promotion soon after and became even more obnoxious. Now he lived in the castle and was responsible for the whole D.M.P. area.

Situated near his office with a clear view of it and of his domicile was a central police telephone exchange with facilities for instant calls to all stations. It was manned by men who had passed exams, were awaiting promotion, and were anxious for good relations with the force. When foxy face left the castle, which he did regularly on surprise 'raids' on stations, an S.O.S. went out to all stations: 'Look out, boys, Reynard left here one minute ago!' On receipt of this danger-signal all ranks jumped into life and bustle. When he arrived everything was shipshape and everybody on the job. On his return the 'all clear' came from the phone office. It was really very comical. To the day he left he never saw through it.

Between himself and Carey there was no love lost. They couldn't stand each other. He directed Carey once to send some data to him in an official memo. I was sent to the castle with the letter. Foxy face complained of the delay (he loved exercising power over lesser folk). Carey sent for me: 'Did you dawdle on the way to the castle, boy?' 'No, Sir, I ran all the way.' 'Ran? Why did you run?' 'Well, Sir, I used to run at home just because I liked to and to get done with the trip!' 'Write that down, boy!' After that I was Carey's white-haired boy: it was not necessary to make any more explanations to an ex-Marathon runner.

Once a week Hurley marched us to the Iveagh baths for swimming lessons. Lessons they could not be called, for we had no teacher. Hurley walked up and down on dry land like Napoleon before Moscow, while we floundered in the pool. One of the lads had a tremendous head of curls of which he was proud. He stood in the shallow end gazing at his reflection, Narcissus-like. This, for some reason, infuriated Hurley, who did not like him. 'Catch that red mop!' he shouted, 'and put it under the water.' The recruit straightened his back and hands on hips replied: 'I'd like

39

to see the man who'd do it!' This, of course, was rank insub-
ordination meriting instant dismissal. Answering back from that
lowest form of life, a recruit, was lethal for him. In a furious
temper, Hurley ordered us out at once and back to the Depot.
Nothing more was heard of the matter. It was known that the
man had influential support amongst the higher-ups.

All this time the Great War raged; now in its last year. Before
I'd left home, my Father, avid for news and with no Sunday
papers, made me cycle ten miles every Sunday to copy an official
British communiqué posted on Abbeyfeale P.O. window. This
usually and naturally gave a slanted version of events and was
optimistic. He subscribed to Hilaire Belloc's magazine, *Land and
Water*, which had long, learned articles about war strategy. The
best comment on Belloc known to me was written by Parkinson
of Parkinson's Law fame: 'Belloc, a conscript Private in the
French Artillery 1912 . . . this made him a strategist.' He was as
good as most of them at the time. At least his articles were
readable.

Upon the Depot wall was an official notice signed Sir John Ross
of Bladensburg. He was the Commissioner in 1916 and resigned
after the rebellion. Only afterwards did I read that Bladensburgh,
a village in America, was the scene of one of the few British
victories in the American Revolutionary War (1814) and gave rise
to their capture of Washington City. His ancestor was made a
baronet after the battle.

They used to say that a constable was carpeted before Ross,
charged with leaving his post of duty. This is a serious offence in
armies and in wartime could merit death. As Sir John had just
left the British Army, he sentenced the man to death. The old
Inspector, horrified, pointed out that in the police, this was but a
trifling offence, for which the penalty was a fine of half-a-crown.
'Very well then,' said Sir John, 'fined half-a-crown.'

Assistant Commissioner Quinn visited the Depot to examine
us in police duties. We paraded in the barrack-square, dressed in
our best. Carey questioned us in turn. This took on an element of
farce, for the whole thing had been rehearsed many times. Each
man knew the question he would be asked, also the answer. Quinn
listened with impassive face to what he must have known was a

40

put-up job. He expressed satisfaction and said we would soon be moving out to our stations. His attitude towards Carey, whom he did not like, was cool but correct.

This transfer was not to be, however, for the so-called 'flu intervened. This was a really terrible disease. Whatever it was, it was not 'flu. It swept the world and was said to have killed more than the war. Attacking the very strongest and fittest of the police, it killed a great number. The onset was very sudden and characterised by a feeling of malaise, high temperature, a raging headache, pains in the back and legs, and a trembling of the whole body. Several of the recruits became desperately ill and I helped to nurse them. One, a nice lad named Shanahan from near Newcastle West, died. The older police were decimated. Grave-diggers worked overtime. Undertakers did a thriving business.

When it was on the wane, it struck me down. Hurley brought me to Meath Hospital, the County Infirmary, in a horse-drawn cab. Ill as I felt, I could not help noticing the mourning *crêpe* on the doors in the poor streets and the continual processions of funerals passing by. It was like the Plague or the Black Death.

Arrived at the hospital we had to wait while three corpses were removed from the lift. My nurse told me later that one had died in my bed. No sooner did I lie down than my nose bled profusely. The awful headache eased somewhat. Sleeping fitfully during the night, the morning found me not too bad. A bearded doctor bent with age came around; he bore the resounding name of Sir John Moore. He looked at my chart: 'My poor fellow! Your nose-bleed saved your life!' Whether or no, it is a fact that slowly recovery came to me. Though as weak as a cat and scarcely able to lift my hands or legs, gradually the illness left me; a shadow of my former self.

The treatment in hospital consisted of anointing the patients' backs with some sort of oil. So every day my pretty namesake, Nurse Neligan, with another, turned me over on my tummy while she rubbed in this oil. In fun she used to call the others to look at the 'giant', acutely embarrassing me. She and the other nurses worked with the utmost devotion, though some of them were only convalescent, badly fed and grossly over-worked. The epidemic had cut down by half the number of nurses. The food was practically non-existent as the kitchen staff was wiped out. But for a poor woman who brought me food from outside I ran a sporting chance of starving. Her brother was in the next bed and she came to visit him every day, bringing him some rations. She gladly accepted when asked to bring me some on my paying for it. Those people, I think, were Quakers; definitely they were Good Samaritans.

In the same ward was a neighbour from home, Maurice Ahern, a D.M.P. man; slowly drawing back from the grave. Having crawled from bed to bed, I used to feed him spoonfuls of milk. Later I gave the nurses a hand at polishing the floors; the wards-maids had departed. Every day, patients died in the ward and the total death-rate for the hospital must have been formidable.

Each police division had a staff-sergeant whose duty included looking after sick men. A Division's Staff-Sergeant Cobbe, a sturdy fellow of cheerful mien from the Midlands, had a sure cure for the so-called 'flu—a diet of whiskey taken neat. He gave the example himself. It is a fact that he did not spend one day in bed—perhaps the germs were asphyxiated by the fumes.

All being unfit for duty, we were left in the Depot for an extra half-year, during which we recruits recruited our strength.

4

ONE DAY in July 1918 Hurley told me to report to Mr Montgomery, Secretary of the D.M.P. at the castle. He was a mild-mannered little Civil Servant with rimless glasses. He showed me a pile of new file boxes and told me to transfer files from old worn-out boxes to them.

I was alone in the musty old room in which I spent two weeks. Those files were nearly all confidential reports on political matters and emanated from the G Division. I read hundreds of them.

The G Division had two wings—one concerned with ordinary crime such as burglary, fraud and theft—the other concerned itself with political subversive movements and was really a secret police. The reports dealt with the Irish Republican Brotherhood, a secret revolutionary society, the Irish Republican Army (originally known as the Volunteers), the Gaelic League bent on restoring the Irish language, and even such harmless organisations as the Irish National Foresters and the Ancient Order of Hibernians.

The latter two were really Catholic Friendly Societies and far from revolutionary. Obviously the Castle feared they might mask dangerous movements. Their web was spread wide and of a fine mesh: they kept a lynx eye on every Irish organisation, big or small, and had done so for hundreds of years. It is well known that for centuries the Castle succeeded in penetrating Irish left-wing circles with the aid of secret services, police, informers, and that crack regiment, St. George's cavalry (i.e. gold sovereigns). The lawyers who 'defended' people like Robert Emmet and John Mitchell were in the secret pay of the Castle. Of course this was not known until many years afterwards.

The British had perfected their espionage system at home and abroad since the time of Walsingham and Cecil. It was the most efficient in the world. A Castle secret service ledger, by some freak, found its way to a second-hand bookstall on the Dublin quays; was there picked up and published by some enterprising citizen. It showed payments of hefty sums (£47,449 for the period 1795–1801) to Irish informers over a long period. The ledger is in the library of the Royal Irish Academy, Dublin. Some informers like Reynolds and Maguire were actually relatives of their victims, and their villainy went undetected for generations.

The G-men had been engaged in political espionage since the time of the Fenians when they were established, and at one time they knew by sight the most dangerous activists; that is true up to and including 1916. After the rebellion in that year they picked out Volunteer and Citizen Army leaders for British firing squads and hundreds more for internment. They served their British masters well.

They used to open mails, watch suspect premises, shadow suspects and had plenty of touts who acted as their eyes and ears. The British infiltrated the I.R.B. in U.S.A. where a man calling himself Le Caron was their spy. He it was who got the Fenian leaders Michael Davitt and Tom Clarke arrested as they did not discover until too late. Le Caron was in the very centre of the Brotherhood.

We know now that the I.R.B. was still in being and only waiting for an opportunity to draw life from the bloody welter of 1916. The leaders of the rebellion had been wiped out by General Maxwell's firing squads. A few remained to carry on the fight. Hundreds of participants and sympathisers had been arrested and deported to Great Britain, but that did not make them more loyal; quite the reverse.

Others were ordered to reside in certain localities, a kind of open arrest. The story is told that when a few of them were ordered to live in Bath, the Parson had the stained-glass windows boarded up! Down at home we had read of those stirring affairs and it was simply history repeating itself: always risings and always beaten.

Overpowering strength, better armaments, sea power, better leaders, ruthlessness and 'St George's Cavalry' on their side. On ours: divided leadership, lack of good leaders (any we threw up like Wellington were on the side of the enemy), and informers always beat us. Never since the Yellow Ford had the Irish won a battle. And not alone were we beaten flat but the same little island had subdued a great part of the globe—the empire on which the sun never set.

The British had many supporters here: the landlords, big business, the banks, the Freemasons, non-Catholics, Castle Catholics, nearly all the rich and educated people. The Catholic Church too, with her supernational outlook and long memory of past persecution was, after Emancipation, far from revolutionary on the whole.

Most of the Irish people, being largely small-holding farmers, were anything but left-wing. All they wanted was a reasonable way of living. The Gladstone Land Acts gave them that. To some extent those measures broke the power of the great landlords whose system was described by the English historian Bryce as the world's worst. Free sale, fixity of tenure and fair rent—the three F's fought for by Davitt and Parnell were granted the farmer tenants.

Yet the landlords still had great estates and influence and through the Kildare Street Club, the Society of Freemasons and the Tory Party dictated to the Castle administration and to the police forces. Nearly all landlords were Protestant, since the so-called Reformation. Through their wealth and power they maintained a stranglehold in the provinces and in the towns also.

Their influence also dominated the courts, through their stipendaries known as Resident Magistrates and the unpaid Justices of the Peace drawn from their ranks.

Lord Clanricarde, a miser and recluse who owned half of Counties Galway and Clare, used to dine in Hyde Park off a ha'penny herring and other courses rescued from dustbins, while his agent in Connaught ground the faces of the tenants. He received sheaves of threatening letters decorated with skull and crossbones. These he transmitted to Clanricarde, who replied: 'My tenants need not think they'll intimidate me by shooting you!' They shot him just the same!

In a village in Loop Head, Co. Clare, the landlord in olden

times evicted anyone allowing Mass to be said in his house. A site for a church could not be got for the same reason. So the people made a kind of covered sedan-chair which they carried on their shoulders to the seashore, the Priest being inside. This was, of course, in the 'bad old days'. The chair, or 'Ark' as it is called, is still preserved in the local church.

Then there was Lord Leitrim in Donegal who claimed to have right over the bodies (*droit de seigneur*) and souls of his tenants until they shot him, though he had an R.I.C. escort. The title died with him.

That day an outside car driven by old Logue, the Cardinal's father, came flying into the village. Old Logue shouted at the top of his voice: 'Lord Leitrim is shot and I lost my whop.'

5

FROM the Depot I was transferred to College Street Police Station, near Trinity College in the city centre. The barracks, a large affair of cut granite, had been then newly opened. It could hold about fifty men.

My first day there produced a lesson in class solidarity. A party was in progress in the canteen which was crowded by men in hilarious mood. Two huge policemen wrestled. One fell on the polished tile floor, breaking a leg. The Superintendent next day asked everyone present for an account of the affair, but nobody said anything. This was the usual form. If the truth had been discovered, both would have been dismissed.

I saw many instances of such 'loyalty'; the police would lie like devils inside and outside court to save a comrade, or when in a tight corner. When collared for any dereliction, a stonewall cure was to 'do the idiot', which nearly always worked. Another was to go sick until the heat went off, or if they were closing in, take refuge in an asylum!

Recruits were issued with new uniforms and other accessories. The winter outfit was very comfortable, with padded tunic. The waterproof coats and cloth capes likewise were of excellent quality and lasted for years. Many found their way to country relations!

The hours of duty were long. Day duty was from 6 a.m. to 9 a.m. and 3 p.m. to 10 p.m. one day, with 9 a.m. to 3 p.m. next day. Night-duty came every three months and the hours were 10 p.m. to 6 a.m. alternating with 7 p.m. to 1 a.m. Helmets were worn then, made of cork, and the 'night hat' had a darkened badge.

Being a novice, a senior man was sent with me at first. A man on beat duty is not to be envied. It is a most boring and monotonous life. The hours pass very slowly especially at night. Often the weather is bad. One gets absolutely jaded. At 4 a.m. the only sound is a sign swinging in the wind or the cry of an alley cat. Often I was on duty at the Central Telephone Exchange which had a garrison of British soldiers. They were quartered in the basement and regularly offered me a cup of char. Never feeling like it at odd hours, I refused, thanking them. The poor English Tommies were always ready to share the little they had.

We were inspected frequently by an inspector or a sergeant on rounds. Our movements were predictable as we followed a route set out in the police beat-book. Often I wished that something would turn up to break the tedium but nothing ever did. The nearest was a shop-breaking in the next beat to mine. This was patrolled by Constable Nolan, a quiet, decent fellow.

A jeweller's shop in the city centre was ransacked; the culprit or his scouts probably timed the job with Nolan's absence from the vicinity. Judge of my surprise when, a few days later, Inspector Barleycorn informed me that Nolan and I were to be carpeted before the Commissioner.

'For what, Sir?' I enquired. 'For neglect of duty in not apprehending the shopbreaker. I advise you to plead guilty!' 'I am not guilty of anything,' I told him, 'and no one will get me to plead guilty.' He went away. Such talk from a recruit was blasphemous!

It was traditional in the service, when a vacancy for a scapegoat turned up, a raw recruit should fill the role, on the somewhat logical ground that he had thirty years to live it down. If he lasted long enough, service would wipe out the blot. There was a saying that 'you'd never be a good policeman until you were "blocked" [i.e. reported] for being drunk, for neglect of duty', and other offences even less reputable.

The day came when Barleycorn warned us to be at the castle with new uniform and polished buttons. He was a suave, oily individual with shifty eyes and a boozy face. At the castle, he again advised me to plead guilty, when I'd get off with a caution, but met with the same answer. Warned by an orderly that the

48

Commissioner would receive us, he yelled: 'Attention! right wheel, quick march!' and other orderly-room slogans.

We found ourselves facing Colonel Johnstone, bland as ever. He had no sword that day or we might have got a swipe like the sheep. Nolan, being senior, was asked what he had to say, but being a timid man, was overawed and remained silent. The Commissioner then said, '46, what have you to say in answer to the charge?' 'I have already told the Inspector, Sir, that I worked my beat that night and do not understand how I came to be charged.' The Inspector's face was crimson. It was unheard of for a recruit to make such a statement or to open his mouth. The Commissioner said: 'Your explanation is accepted.' Nolan was cautioned and we left, Barleycorn being told to remain behind. Afterwards he told his pals I had influence with the Commissioner and gave me a wide berth.

Often, I patrolled the south quays with a senior man. At one street corner a flourishing pitch and toss 'school' was in progress. This was illegal under some old Act, perhaps the V Victoria which gave wide power to the Dublin police. Senior used to wait until the kitty on the ground contained a fair sum. Then he directed me to go round the back to cut them off while he ran straight at them. They cleared off and he pocketed the money. Years afterwards we met. 'You owe me a lot of money!' 'How's that, Dave?' Half those kitties you stole off the toss school.' He laughed heartily. Joking aside, though, we were lucky that those fellows took it so well. Perhaps they regarded the police as a necessary evil like their bosses. They never showed us any hostility.

I was sent to South George's Street on duty alone one day. It is a busy shopping centre. Three or four little girls with parcels ran down a lane when they saw me. I followed and found they had a lot of things such as silver-backed toilet accessories and other new objects which perhaps were the proceeds of shop-lifting. I brought them to the station accompanied by the usual throng of idlers. The Station Sergeant got their names and addresses. Divisional Detective Sergeant 'Johnny' Barton took over.

Cadaverous, immensely tall with weird clothes and farmer's

49

boots he looked like a Rustic from an Abbey play. Anyone would take him for a simpleton but it would be a major error. He was easily the best detective in these islands, had plenty of touts working for him and was known to be well-off financially. At that time numbers of Britons evading conscription were hiding in Dublin. They were known as Flyboys and some had plenty of money. Anyway they had more money than a desire to fight. Johnny, with his marvellous ring of touts quickly got on their track. The next step was a call on the reluctant warrior. It was said that, for a consideration, they were left in peace. However that may be, and it may be a canard, Barton and I took those children to their room in a poor tenement. It was a tall old building. Johnny questioned the mother but could get nothing out of her. She was a tough 'oul' wan'. He started to shake her. Getting bored with this performance which led nowhere, I decided to go to the top floor and gape at the scenery. When I got to the next landing I saw a grown girl with two large sacks which proved to be crammed with new stolen articles. Johnny's eyes popped when he saw them. The old woman was arrested. I was commended for good police duty and received a couple of pounds from a reward fund. Amusingly enough, this reward fund is fed from fines inflicted on the police for breaches of discipline; feeding the dog with his own tail, as it were. Barton was so charmed that he asked me into a pub. It was a warm day. 'What'll you have?' 'A bottle of lemonade.' He ordered one. 'Aren't you going to drink?' I asked him. 'No, I don't drink.' So we walked out. He made money legitimately through carrying out various assignments for city shopkeepers, sometimes to watch their wives! I've seen many messages for Barton, no one else would do. Some time later Superintendent Brien of the G Division asked Barton to join that unit. They wanted to use him against the I.R.A. and promised him promotion. He consulted two Cork brothers named Forrest who had long service in the G: one was an inspector and the other a sergeant. They warned him to keep out of it. But the lure of promotion, money and his docile attitude to his superiors gained the upper hand. He joined. In quick time he discovered a little dump of arms. The Castle was jubilant; Barton would soon show them! He was shot soon afterward.

We were about to go on duty the night of 13th Septemebr 1919 at 10 p.m. when there was a rattle outside the door as if someone were running a stick across iron railings. On going out we saw a man lying in the street. He had been shot. He was Detective Sergeant Hoey whom I'd often seen at S.F. meetings. He was a smart-looking fellow of thirty, flashily dressed. Engaged in a race for promotion with Detective Sergeants Smyth and Bruton (not to be confused with Barton), he now met his end. So did Smyth. Bruton got the promotion and sat out the war in the castle.

Each man in my station had a cubicle. My neighbour George Connolly was a stout, toughly built man from the West coast. Sometimes, when off duty, I used to lie on my bed reading. George used to give the wooden partition a violent kick with his army boot and shout, 'Are you studyin', 46 you cute basket, you want to get on in the job.' He and I and Phil Lennon used to play handball for hours in the ball-alley at the rear.

Another time, the three of us would walk to Dalkey and back, a round trip of about ten miles. We did this training at least once a week, to keep fit. Some policemen took no exercise, and soon their health failed.

There was a monthly kit inspection by the Superintendent. One man had no kit except an undershirt which was as black as the ace of spades. It had been white once, a heck of a long time ago. As the Superintendent left the cubicle next to blackshirt's, the kit came flying over the partition and was duly inspected for the second time. It was a mere matter of form, just another regulation, not to be taken seriously.

Once I saw a wild rush by police out of the station. I asked one where was the fire and he replied, 'Nowhere. They are going to warn a street bookmaker that he is to be raided.' All police followed racing.

George's beat was always the South quays where he was quite popular in spite of his usual greetings to toughs: 'I'll break you up!' Those port workers were all members of Connolly's and Larkin's Union. They had no love for the police. This sprang from the labour lock-out and ensuing riots in 1913. The Union was then in its infancy and fought the wretched wages and conditions in Dublin notably in the Dublin Tramway Co. The

Castle, always on the side of the rich, fought the Union tooth and nail. They drafted hundreds of R.I.C. into the city where baton charges were the order of the day and of the night also. The R.I.C. were even more unpopular than the D.M.P.

James Connolly, the Irish Lenin, formed the Irish Citizen Army, a kind of radical unit to back up the workers. After the 1916 rebellion in which he took a leading part and in which he was gravely wounded, a British firing squad propped him up in a chair and put an end to his life. A very dangerous man to capitalists! The Dublin Fire Brigade also was unfriendly to the police, they too were on the radical side and always surly to the force.

An amusing police regulation was one that ordered you to bed at a reasonable hour, I think 11 p.m. 'Losing your rest' was an offence, the theory being that a sleepy policeman would not protect the citizens' property! A joke was that a lazy fellow would be up for losing his rest. If anything went wrong, one could be quite sure that comrades would be struck blind. Wild horses would not drag an admission out of them. I've heard blatant perjury in the courts to save a comrade, and seen files consisting of atrocious lies. Nearly all the officers were decent enough and there was no ill-feeling between the ranks.

There were, of course, a few crooks who should have been in jail, but where is the force which has not got them? The code of regulations was so stiff that an officer could easily make a man's life a hell, but I never saw that happen. In this they were sup-posed to differ from the R.I.C. who often reported one another. I knew an R.I.C. man who unhorsed an inspector and a head constable! Curiously enough, he was a mild sort of fellow to speak to, but apparently a terror with a pen! Having a sound knowledge of the code, he was able to pick holes in those fellows. Three or four men cooped up in a little cross-roads station were, I suppose, bound to get on one another's nerves eventually.

Examinations were held for promotion to various D.M.P. ranks. Certificates were issued to successful candidates, and that for sergeant's rank was known as the dog licence. A senior man of my acquaintance went to a grinder to prepare for this examina-tion. On his return from a session he was asked how he was getting on. 'Well,' says he, 'English is bloody hard—I can understand "to", "two", but blast me if I know what "too" means.' However, he got the exam and was promoted. The subtleties of the language, however, still evaded him: when reading a report for men going on duty he recited: 'Stolen from a field in Terenure, one EWEE.' He made two syllables of it—ramming it home as it were. We had another man who was famed for his efforts to explain things. He was in court one day as he had accompanied a sergeant in a raid on a pub. Drinking after authorised hours was in progress. The publican was prosecuted. There was a question as to how much liquor was in a certain glass on the counter. Conflicting statements having been made, the Beak appealed to our friend. 'It was most full, yer Worship,' he said. This not serving to elucidate the problem he added: 'It was as high up as it was low down.' This quip proved so successful that everyone laughed including himself. A student gave him his visiting card and when an inspector asked him who the man was, he said, 'He's a T.C.D. out of Trinity College, Sir'.

In the old days the Dublin police and the R.I.C. were very badly paid. In 1913 their wages were 12s. per week. It was astonishing that a lot of the old D.M.P. owned house-property and were slum landlords. Of course a share of this could be put down to graft, scrounging presents and other favours, and plain roguery; habits not confined to the police of this island. In London police circles it was known as pulling tradesmen's ears. Dublin police travelled free on the tramway system, the owner being grateful for service rendered in the labour troubles of 1913, I suppose.

The Great War had thrown a great deal of extra work on the Dublin police. My station being in the city centre was one of the busiest. Often at night, the Station Sergeant on duty would tell me to remain behind to help in the office instead of going on a beat. This did not sit too well with the senior men; it was a soft job and naturally enough they thought should be their prerogative. Though they groused a bit and called me a so and so raw recruit, that was the extent of their hostility.

Earlier, I referred to the Castle's fear of such innocuous bodies as the Ancient Order of Hiberians, a society friendly to

Redmond's parliamentary party. Before I joined the police, someone persuaded the D.M.P. to join this body which promised to agitate for higher wages and better conditions for them. In the Police Manual (the Bible of the force), as I've said, it was laid down that for the police membership of any society excepting that of Freemasons, was strictly prohibited. So the Castle instantly forbade the police joining the A.O.H. and sent out instructions to that effect. The police ignored the order and attended meetings at the A.O.H. hall in Parnell Square, Dublin. The Castle sent inspectors and superintendents to the hall to take their names. They enlisted the help of tramway employees to report on personnel travelling to the city on the nights when meetings were held. Ringleaders amongst the police, notably Hetherington and Murray, were picked out and ordered on transfer to Dalkey, the Siberia of the D.M.P. This is a pleasant little township on the edge of the Irish Sea. It has always baffled me why the Castle pinpointed it as a penal station but such was the case. Life could pass like a dream in Dalkey. In fact, at times it was my regret that I was not sent there! The men ordered on transfer hired a hearse and a number of mourning carriages. The bier was loaded with their regulation boxes and drawn by black horses with nodding plumes. Their friends and sympathisers filled the cabs. An immense throng of idlers, laughing and jeering, followed the procession. The Castle was furious. Some leaders were fined and transferred. Hetherington and Murray were sacked. Thus the Castle defeated the Dublin police and perhaps punished them for not complying with the Code by joining the Society of Freemasons! This did nothing to make the administration more loved by the police, already neutral as far as the revolution was concerned.

An R.I.C. sergeant named T. J. McElligott, a Kerryman, was an ardent sympathiser with Sinn Fein and made no secret of it. He was sacked after an altercation with a squireen about a rebel flag. It appears that this petty landlord ordered him to take down the emblem and he refused. The landlords 'owned' the R.I.C. He got in touch with Collins and became a sort of agitator and organiser of the R.I.C. Ostensibly working to improve their pay and conditions of service, he really was bent on breaking up the force, or rendering it harmless and was financed by Collins. He came to a mass meeting of Dublin police. I went along. The hall was crowded. McElligott, a handsome looking man, made an impressive harangue. He had a glib tongue.

A union for police and prison officers had come into being. At this time (Summer, 1918) or shortly afterwards, both Irish police forces and the prison warders were within measurable distance of a strike. About 99 per cent of the Dublin police were in the union. Excitement and enthusiasm ran high at the meeting. Somebody in the body of the hall asked: 'Were the G-men in the union?' (What he meant was: are the G-men carrying out their traditional role of spies; this time on their comrades.) A G-sergeant named Broy was on the platform with another G-man named Kavanagh. Broy answered the question (with tongue in cheek). 'Every decent man in the G Division is in the union,' says he. The following morning the old Superintendent 'Butt' Brien came into the office where Broy and Kavanagh worked. He saluted them by saying: 'I wonder who are the decent men in this job?' The usual snake-in-the-grass had turned up! An elderly constable came to our station at this time from Kevin Street. At the same time a message arrived via the bush telegraph: he had refused to join the union. He stayed only two days during which he was boycotted. No one spoke to him or would eat or drink with him. An English-born sergeant named Beggs, though a Freemason and loyalist, was a staunch union man and organiser. The Castle, terrified of the spectre of a police strike, sent for Beggs and other union men and granted their demands.

A Royal Commission under the chairmanship of Lord Desborough was set up to enquire into questions of pay, etc., of police in Great Britain and Ireland. This eventually recommended fairly substantial increases. The union fell apart and became a complete flop: so did McElligott's scheme. The R.I.C. turned away from Sinn Fein. The London police were actually on strike at the time of McElligott's meeting. Collins sent him to interview their leaders and Liam Tobin, Collins' principal intelligence officer, went with him, as they both told me afterwards. One day while McElligott was at London police strike H.Q. a visitor was announced. He told them he was Jameson, an Englishman. He was Chief Delegate of the Soldiers', Sailors' and Airmen's Union to which all the British fighting forces belonged. He came to tell them that those forces were right behind the London police. They would not lift a finger against them. The strikers thanked him effusively for this splendid display of fraternal solidarity. He was a nicely dressed man of middle age and a wonderful, persuasive, impassioned speaker. Having been introduced to McElligott, the delegate from Ireland, he started to question him as to the Irish police situation. McElligott was about to reply when his eye caught Jack Hayes, the 'policeman's M.P.'. Hayes stood behind Jameson's back with his finger to his lips. McElligott therefore made some innocuous reply. The London strikers had been warned by those in a position to know that Jameson was a secret service man come as a spy. We shall meet him again later.

So far as Collins and Sinn Fein were concerned, this union business was a dead loss as Collins had hoped to break up the police forces in Ireland in that way. When those men got the increased wages they turned their backs on McElligott and on the union and incidentally on Sinn Fein. To give the R.I.C. their due, though, they gave McElligott a substantial sum as some recompense for his services. Later, he had to go 'on the run', being threatened with internment, or worse, death.

Single men in the Dublin police lived in barracks; married men were allowed to live outside. The same thing applied in the G Division, whose ranks were always filled from the uniformed force. Promotion was very slow in both of these organisations, and generally vacancies occurred only on retirement. Bruton won the race for promotion and was given a house at the castle gate. He sat out the war in the castle and was made Chief Inspector. Zeal in political duty led to promotion, unfortunately to sudden death also, at that time. Bruton was lucky or had someone's prayers.

'Count' O'Connor, 199B, was the oldest man in College Station and had a soft job as jailor, whose duty it was to look after any prisoners in the three cells there. He received his 'title' through the splendour of his dress, his courtly appearance and his perfect manners. Perhaps titles have been awarded on less noble grounds? Anyway, he was a charming character and great

56

company. A native of Abbeyfeale, Co. Limerick, he was a neighbour of mine at home and had been in the force for thirty years at least. He was about six feet six inches in height, of portly build, had a red face (from copious libations), an immense waxed moustache. He spoke like the perfect gentleman he was. Welcomed in the best society, he was friendly with eminent lawyers, surgeons and other prominent citizens. Always ready to do a good turn, there was never a time when he had not several projects on hands; get a job for this man, get a girl into a hospital as a nurse at a reduced fee, or square some bit of trouble for someone else. No one could refuse him anything in reason. Sketchily educated, like the rest of us, he was a wonderful talker. Always very well dressed, I've seen him wearing a fur-collared overcoat and looking more like a magnate than a P.C. An Irish Brummel!

The story went that a new Chief Secretary arrived in Dublin years before. This was a key-rank in the Administration and next in importance to the Viceroy. He attended the Dublin Horse Show, a display of fashion, and was promenading there with two companions. The D.M.P. Commissioner and the Chief Superintendent, both well down in the Castle pecking order, were looking on. The Commissioner enquired from his colleague: 'Who is the distinguished gentleman with the rolled umbrella?' 'That's 199B, Sir.' 'Ridiculous!' he snorted, 'Have him transferred to Dalkey at once!' He thought better of it, though. The 'Count' finished out his time at College Station. Another time he was holidaying in Ballybunion, a pleasant Kerry resort, where our Captain assumed the prone. His feminine companion, an Australian, expressed a wish to see the British fleet, then exercising off that coast. The 'Count', ever ready to oblige, sent a telegram to the Admiral at Queenstown, signed Count O'Connor. The Admiral, not having Debrett handy, hastily complied. A tender arrived off the coast and embarked the 'Count' and his party who were suitably entertained on board the flagship.

When he was a young man, on duty one night, he was invited by the cook to the kitchen of a nice house in St Stephen's Green. It was the home of a crusty old bachelor lawyer. The 'Count' was enjoying a nice snack when they heard a door open. He hid in the pantry. A bell rang in the kitchen. When the servant answered

57

she was asked: 'Is there a man in the kitchen?' 'What would a man be doing there, Sir?' she replied. 'Go to bed at once!' The 'Count' had been warned when going on duty to pay special attention to the house of the Inspector-General of the R.I.C., a few doors away, which was vacant. On his way out of the rear of the lawyer's house he found a ladder by which he reached the street. He should have gone off duty hours before but pretended that he feared burglars were in the I.G.'s house. Later he was told to report to the Superintendent's office. Quaking, he feared all had been discovered. The Superintendent clapped him on the back. 'Son, I'm going to recommend you for good police duty; you frightened the burglar last night; he came back this morning and swiped the I.G.'s silver!' Years passed. When he came on duty one night the Station Sergeant told him that a well-known burglar named Smith was in the cell. He was the man who had robbed the I.G. The 'Count' gave him three pints of stout. He got so drunk that he could not be brought before the Magistrate until next day. The 'Count' got him off on the plea that he was going to reform, also that he would get the poor old wretch a job.

6

IN THE autumn of 1919 the castle called for recruits from the uniformed force for the G Division. Being heartily tired of uniform and beat duty, I applied and was accepted. This was due to no merit on my part as the shootings had made this service unpopular with the general run of the force. In peace times it was difficult to get in but now the opposite was the case. The Castle was faced with a tough situation. Never before had such a determined and lethal attack been made on the British intelligence forces nor one directed with such ruthless efficiency.

We were received by Superintendent 'Butt' Brien. The Irish have a felicity for nicknames. A butt is a large cask, also a dung-cart. Brien was about five feet high and perhaps three in girth. He had a round closed pussy-cat's face and little piggy eyes. Weighing about fourteen stone he had suave oily manners. On meeting him, my reaction was—beware! He told us we would soon wipe out the gunmen, and made other soothing remarks. They said he had been a pawnbroker's assistant before he joined forty years earlier. Seeing that G-men were recruited solely from uniform it was astonishing how he got in owing to his lack of height and more astonishing that he had attained his present rank. Of course, in his heyday he had to contend with only a handful of conspirators. As he was full of low cunning, he probably succeeded in riddling them with spies. One thing is certain. He did not receive promotion from the Castle for nothing. Like a stage Chinaman, he was forever 'washing' his pudgy little hands, while those little eyes surveyed your face. Poor devils like Tom Clarke, M. Davitt, O'Donovan Rossa and Connolly were easy meat for the 'Butt'. Now he was really up against it, and soon to be pushed out on pension. He and his men had picked out leaders after the 1916 rebellion for British firing squads and he would do so again if he got the chance. He lived just outside the castle gate. His only relaxation was to attend the Royal music hall, which he did every night, sitting in the front row admiring the chorus girls' legs.

I was only a few days in the G Division when he ordered me and another man to accompany him on a trip to the north side of the city. We went in a horse-drawn cab and when we came to Gardiner Place he told us to wait while he went into a small boarding house or private hotel. We were his escort. He was getting afraid for his life, and with reason! Needless to say he did not confide in us, but from various bits and pieces of information I concluded he was visiting a spy known as Quinlisk. This man, who was the only one of that name I've ever heard of, was an ex-soldier of the British Army and of Casement's Irish Brigade. For some months he had been haunting S.F. circles in an effort to obtain money, and on being turned down, took up relations with the Castle. A letter he wrote to Brien was intercepted, in which he offered to trap Michael Collins, whom he called a scoundrel. This sealed his fate. He was sent on a wild-goose chase to Cork and shot there by the volunteers, on 18th February 1920.

Needless to say, I was not going to stick my neck out for the Castle and Mr Brien; all I wanted was a soft job. So far as pay was concerned, G-men received a pittance of a few shillings a week more than the ordinary police, and the Castle, stingily enough, did nothing about improving it. If there were any attractions they consisted of freedom from uniform, from night duty and the tedium of street duty. Brien's predecessor, Mallon, away back in 1882, had discovered the killers of Cavendish and Burke (two high Castle officials) in the Phoenix Park. By means of an old police trick—pretending that his comrades had betrayed him—he got one of the party to confess and turn Queen's evidence. The Castle subsequently sent the informer to Australia, but he was shot on board ship by an Irishman. The slayers of Burke and his friend were a kind of left-wing splinter-group calling themselves the Invincibles.

We were issued with a ·38 automatic pistol such as we had used

60

in the Depot. It is a small weapon and had a bad fault, being liable to jam. I used it only twice: once it discharged in my pocket as I was fooling with it, thereby frightening the wits out of two old detective inspectors. Looking down, I saw my pocket on fire, so I cleared out of the room in Brunswick Street (now Pearse Street) where those men were writing a report. A Black and Tan held me up to rob me so I let fly at him. This was much later, of course.

All the G-men at that time were housed in Brunswick Street except the Superintendent whose office was in the castle. About twelve or fifteen others joined with me. Shortly afterwards we, the political branch, moved to the castle leaving behind those engaged in ordinary police or detective duty. It was clear to the Castle that leakages were going on and somehow they thought by this move to defeat them. Perhaps they thought that Pearse Street was in too open a situation and so comings and goings could be watched by political enemies. Pierce Beasley seemed under the impression that G-men were exclusively employed on political work, but this was not the case; only a handful were so engaged. All left in Brunswick Street were engaged in investigating ordinary offences.

7

DUBLIN CASTLE is an immense unwieldy pile built by King John (of Magna Carta fame) 1167–1216. It has no claim to architectural beauty, having neither shape nor distinction. It was always the centre of British rule in Ireland, the Irish Bastille. The walls weep, not for the sins of the inhabitants, but because of a fault in the stone. The little river Poddle runs underneath and the whole place is damp, dark, smells of age and mould. It was a prison in ages past. It was from its Birmingham tower that Red Hugh O'Donnell and his companions escaped in 1591. They had been kidnapped by Elizabeth's Lord Deputy Perrott. Hostages were held there for different reasons of state. As Mrs Stopford Green, famed Irish historian, says in *The Making of Ireland and its Undoing* (Macmillan 1908): '. . . For centuries it remained the English system to train up or to single out for wealth and reward, the most ignoble of the race, men greedy, dishonest, unnatural and treacherous. Such men can be found in any country. . . . Children were sent as pledges to Dublin Castle. Sydney and Sussex carried off . . . every notable chief's son they could lay hands on.'

The castle is divided roughly in half by two yards known as Upper and Lower. The former contained the offices of the Chief and Under Secretaries and their assistants. These were the real rulers of Ireland under the nominal head, the Lord Lieutenant or Viceroy, who lived in the Viceregal Lodge, Phoenix Park, a couple of miles away. The Under Secretaries lived in the park also. The Upper yard also contained the Heraldry office. From here were stolen in 1907 the Irish Crown Jewels. Neither the jewels nor the culprit were discovered. It was an early whodunit. The theft, if such it was, came to light on the eve of a royal visit

62

Michael Collins and O'Reilly.
Photo: Independent Newspapers
Ltd.

POLICE NOTICE.

£1000 REWARD

WANTED FOR MURDER IN IRELAND.

DANIEL BREEN

(calls himself Commandant of the Third
Tipperary Brigade).

Age 27, 5 feet 7, inches in height, bronzed complexion, dark hair (long in front), grey eyes, short cocked nose, stout build, weight about 12 stone, clean shaven ; sulky bulldog appearance : looks rather like a blacksmith coming from work ; wears cap pulled well down over face.

The above reward will be paid by the Irish Authorities, to any person not in the Public Service who may give information resulting in his arrest.
Information to be given at any Police Station.

Police notice concerning Daniel
Breen, issued in January 1919.

Removal of the bodies of Treacy and Price and the scene of the shooting.

by King Edward. Later, a Royal Commission of Enquiry was held which, as usual, published nothing of any value. After some hocus pocus, the custodian of the regalia, Sir Arthur Vicars, was sacked. He went to live near Listowel, Co. Kerry. There he was shot by raiders on 14th April 1921. Whoever shot him, presumably it was not the Volunteers, for their G.H.Q. took the unusual step of denying responsibility. There were, of course, plenty of criminals taking advantage of the troubles to suit themselves. The identity of his killers remains a mystery to this day, just as does his part in the disappearance of those baubles.

There are state apartments in the Upper yard; also a magnificent ballroom where the bucks and belles of old disported during the castle season. Some of the rooms have fine furniture and hangings and a couple of Bossi mantlepieces.

The Lower yard contained the H.Q.'s of the D.M. Police and the R.I.C.; the British Army's Dublin Command, the Birmingham Tower containing state archives, and the Chapel Royal. This latter has carvings by Grinling Gibbons, 1648–1721. It is now a Catholic church. Each window of the chapel contains a representation of the coats of arms of two Viceroys. Curiously enough, the last half-window is filled with the arms of the last Viceroy, Lord Fitzalan.

In the Lower yard was also a police station of the uniformed D.M.P., a central telephone exchange, and the house of the Chief Superintendent. The castle had a military garrison who manned each gate, strengthened by steel plates since 1916. When things got hot, a pass was necessary to enter. Later, a company of Police Auxiliaries arrived and took up quarters inside the lower gate at Exchange Court. The police offices were cramped and shabby. Space was at a premium owing to the disturbed state of the country. This situation grew worse as time went on, for hordes of officials lived in terror of their lives, and had to be accommodated there, never leaving the place day or night.

A symbolical figure of Justice graces the Upper yard and faces into the quadrangle; Daniel O'Connell remarked that she had turned her backside to the citizens.

We had a little messroom with elderly women cooks. The bedrooms contained two beds. My room-mate, a quiet, decent

63

poor ex-medical student named Fox, suffered from tuberculosis which soon killed him. We went to his funeral in the Midlands. He must have contracted the disease since joining, for old Dr Oulton was very strict on that.

An inspector named McFeely was in charge of us, but was soon sacked. He was from the North, and often I escorted him to his home at night as he went in fear of his life. Here is the explanation of his dismissal. The British fired Assistant Commissioner Quinn out on pension. He was too wise to tangle with Sinn Fein. To fill his job they brought Detective Inspector Redmond, R.I.C. from Belfast. All the G-men were ordered to parade one night in November, 1919, in Brunswick Street. We were addressed by Redmond. He was a neatly-built man of about forty, nattily dressed and wearing a bowler. He looked more like a stockbroker than a policeman. He gave us a pep talk. It was extraordinary, he said, that we, who knew Dublin so well, could not catch Michael Collins, whereas a man who had only just arrived from England had managed to meet him more than once.

Though I did not then know the mysterious visitor to whom he referred, it was later made clear to me. The man from England was the secret-service man who had told the London police strikers that the armed services would not lift a finger against them, he representing their Soldiers' Sailors' and Airmen's Union. Through some third party, probably a London Sinn Feiner named Art O'Brien, he arranged to meet Michael Collins, to whom he told the same story. Collins was inclined to believe him but Tom Cullen, one of his best intelligence men, warned him that he was a crooked Englishman. Cullen was wrong, but only about his nationality; he was the son of a district inspector in the R.I.C. from (of all places) Newcastle West. Apparently he was a star secret-service operator, with that blend of audacity, eloquence, and three o'clock in the morning courage required in this service. His real name was Burns*. Several times he had interviews with Collins, Tobin and Cullen. He lunched with Collins at the home of Batt O'Connor, a faithful friend of Collins. How true that nations suffer most from their sons who go over to the enemy! It must be said that this man was really smart.

* In Ireland, he called himself Jameson. See p. 55.

The union of which Burns told the London police and which he now trotted out to Collins was, of course, purely a figment of his imagination. To convince Collins, he handed to Cullen a suit-case full of revolvers. Cullen, a gay, quick-witted fellow, walked with him down O'Connell Street carrying the guns. He told Burns: 'I'm going to leave them in this shop—it's a dump for us,' indicating a well-known tobacconist's at the corner of O'Connell Bridge. He said 'So long' to Burns and went through the door, leaving through one around the corner, still carrying the case. So Burns saw his British contact and told him where to pick up these weapons. (The British, of course, had no desire to arm the I.R.A.!)

Inspector McFeely was sent to raid the shop, found nothing and was promptly sacked. This incident should have displayed the warning light for Burns, but his audacity outweighed his good sense. He'd actually told Collins that he'd get him arms from Russia! Assistant Commissioner Redmond did not show us his hand. He brought from Belfast a squad of picked R.I.C. detectives who did not appear at any Dublin police station, but lived about the city as civilians. Redmond worked closely with Burns. The former made a serious blunder, though. It was to cost the lives of both. Of all the G-men, he picked as his guide Jas. McNamara, who lately had been enrolled by Collins as one of his agents. McNamara was an attractive personality and very smart. Redmond brought McNamara with him raiding Batt O'Connor's house looking for Collins and listening to conversation outside. McNamara of course warned Collins; but for that he was a goner. It was the most vital service ever rendered to Collins, for Burns certainly went very near to having him in the net! Once, Redmond told Mrs O'Connor that he would not trouble her again. This was a strange thing to say. It is not clear why he said it. But it turned out to be right. He was shot* a few nights later when on his way to his hotel in Harcourt Street. It is clear that he under-estimated Collins' inroads in the ranks of the Castle G-men. He had actually made McNamara his confidential clerk and trusted aide. Needless to say his squad from Belfast left here hurriedly.

* A reward of £10,000 was offered by the British on 25th January, 1920 for information on the killers. No one claimed it.

They certainly showed good judgement thereby! If Burns had not been warned by earlier events, Redmond's death should have clinched it; if he had any sense left he should have made a bee-line for the mail boat. But he didn't! That audacity which had brought him through former crises now prompted him to dice with death. After all that had happened, Collins seemed strangely reluctant to kill him, even though it was plain as a pikestaff that he was a spy and furthermore an *agent provocateur*. So Collins warned his staff to keep away from Burns. Probably he hoped he would go away. One night in February 1920 when Joe O'Reilly, Collins' courier, was stopped by Burns in the street, Joe trembled at the thought of the dressing-down Collins would give him for talking to him. Joe was asked by Burns to make an appointment with Collins for him, and this he promised to do. Burns used all the persuasive powers which he possessed in great measure. When O'Reilly told Collins, he was terribly annoyed. 'I'll show him!' he said and gave O'Reilly a note to Tobin. O'Reilly met Burns next night and sent him off with two men 'to meet Collins'. They shot Burns. He bluffed to the last, but the forfeit had to be paid. His luck had run out. I think he was the last agent to try the personal approach. His employers must have found it difficult to get people for such a mission.

Redmond's vacancy was advertised throughout the R.I.C. An inspector took the job, but did not go looking for trouble and was not interfered with. Actuated by curiosity, I attended Redmond's inquest at the Meath Hospital where his body had been brought. Later, the British forbade inquests as juries had brought in verdicts of murder against Crown forces, and even against Lloyd George and his government, when persons had been killed by their forces. They wanted the jury in this case to bring in a verdict of wilful murder. This they did not achieve. The police had the job of choosing the jury. There were few sympathisers with Sinn Fein on it!

The Crown was represented by a young barrister who made a blustering speech which had no effect on the jury. I heard him at an inquest on Martin Savage, a Volunteer killed in an un-successful attack on Lord French which occurred on 19th December 1919. This time he cross-examined a poor devil of a British

66

captain: 'Why didn't you take steps to cut off the assassins', etc. There was something nauseous in listening to this chancer, who simply wanted to impress his paymasters in the Castle. Need I add that he graced the bench soon afterwards?

We had a few Orangemen in the G Division. Most of them were not bad fellows, but one or two had all the hallmarks of the brethren. In the Depot a few of us used to say the Rosary at bed-time until Carey stopped it. Those fellows must have assumed that I was out to convert them! One morning I saw painted on a wall in the castle in letters a foot tall: NELIGAN, SPY FOR THE POPE. As I knew the scribe had a slate off, this did not bother me. Those men were completely at sea here. As instruments for the Castle, they were an entire failure, yet on account of their alleged, much paraded loyalty they received promotion in the police, but certainly not on merit. Singling them out was part of the discrimination rife in that régime.

Chief Inspector Bruton ordered me early in 1920 to go on a raid to 76 Harcourt Street, where the illegal Dail, or Sinn Fein administration, had an office. We were accompanied by British soldiers. I knew that a neighbour, Paddy Sheehan, worked there so I went upstairs and counted the roses on the wallpaper until the raid was over. All the staff including Sheehan were arrested and got a few months in prison. (The British knew it was useless bringing them before a jury who would acquit them, so they had them tried summarily and sentenced by a paid magistrate who would do as he was told. That is what he was getting paid for!) An immense amount of Dail stationary was seized on that raid. It was afterwards used by the Auxiliaries for sending threatening letters to S.F. leaders! Later, I saw piles of it in their office in the castle.

8

ABOUT this time, my brother Maurice visited me
and persuaded me to resign, which I did on 11th May 1920. I was
sick of the job at the time anyway. As the P.P. would not give him
a vacancy in my Father's school (nor one to my sister, who had
to go to Co. Tipperary), he threw up teaching altogether. He became an organiser for the Irish Transport and General Workers'
Union; based on Tralee. An able organiser and a trenchant
speaker, he soon made things hum. A lot of poor wretches were
slaving in small shops and factories for coolie wages in those days,
and were strictly forbidden to join a union. In these days it is
scarcely credible, but such was the case. Maurice, a fine-looking
man with the build of an athlete, who was genuinely interested
in human welfare, went to all those places and interviewed the
workers, telling them of the advantages of being organised. At
one small creamery he was addressing the staff at lunch-hour
when the proprietor, a huge man, arrived and seizing a shovel,
threatened him and ordered him to clear out. Maurice put his
hand in his (empty) hip-pocket and said: 'Drop that shovel or
I'll blow your brains out!' The man complied, and not only did
the staff join the union, but they went on strike there and then.

I resigned from the police. Before I left I went to Bru nswick
Street to say good-bye to my friends. I met Detective La rry
Dalton with whom I'd often gone to the Broadstone Railway
terminus on duty. Dalton was also from West Limerick and a
stout man of about thirty. A charming fellow of mild disposition,
he had never raised a finger against Sinn Fein, except for one
incident. G-men went to the house of a well-known Sinn Feiner
named J. J. Walsh in Dublin to arrest him. Dalton was sent to the

rear. Walsh ran out the back door and tried to persuade Dalton to let him go, but he would not. The day I was leaving I met Dalton and he asked me to go up to the Broadstone to say good-bye to our friends there. This was not possible as my train-time was near. That very day or the next he was shot dead on his way to the Broadstone. The man who was with him ran away. I attended his funeral at Monegay and met his brother, a member of the Volunteers, and other relatives. An acquaintance came up to me and said: 'I believe he used to dress up as a priest to catch the boys.' 'It is a damned lie,' I replied and turned away in disgust. All that can be said now is that personal antagonism brought about this man's death, which I deeply regret. It was one of the tragedies of the time.

A man named Tim Kennedy who was Accountant for Kerry County Council told Maurice he wanted to see me. I went from my home to Tralee where we met him in his office in Ashe Street. Kennedy was a tiny fellow with cherubic face, very bright eyes, and was a clever fellow. Like many more at that time, he was leading a Jekyll and Hyde life—a neutral by day and an active and efficient Brigade Intelligence Officer by night. Later, I got to know him very well; we became close friends and so remained to the day of his death many years later. He told me that Collins wanted to see me, and that he wanted me to go back to the G Division to work for him. Before I resigned I had seen Paddy Sheehan, who was on the Dail staff and was sometime private secretary to De Valera, and had offered my services. Sheehan promised to enquire, returned and advised me to resign. Kennedy now told me that this was done without Collins' knowledge: that he would never have allowed me to resign. After some further conversation I agreed to go to Dublin to meet him. I suggested to Kennedy that he should arrange for a few threatening letters to be sent to me at home in Limerick, ordering me to clear out, and I could show them to the Castle people. These duly arrived. Curiously enough they were the only samples I've ever received, though sending them is a pastime in Ireland. It appeared that Sheehan, who belonged then to the political wing of Sinn Fein, had not realised the implications of my offer. Collins was annoyed that he had not been told. At this time the war here was going full blast. The R.I.C. had retreated into sand-bagged barracks in the larger towns. Unpaid magistrates had resigned wholesale, some under duress. The British Government writ had ceased to run and reposed on the bayonet.

Then, or soon, whole provinces were in the grip of martial law which seriously incommoded non-combatants. The country was being ground between the opposing terrors of British and Volunteer rule. For, let there be no mistake, one was no less real than the other. A kind of madness had seized the nation; a situation since painfully familiar across the world.

I was preparing for the trip to Dublin when a terrible tragedy befell us. Maurice left home one evening to go to a religious Mission in Abbeyfeale. He rode a motor-cycle, and my sister Eileen was on the pillion. Fifteen minutes after they had left, I heard a motor-car and a neighbour beckoned to me. It was Ml. O'Mahony, the manager of our creamery. He told me that there had been an accident and he was coming for the Priest. We went to the scene. The front wheel of the machine had hit a stone of a bridge over a river at a bend, and a sliver of stone had penetrated Maurice's skull. He was thrown on the road, breathing with a loud snoring sound. I knew enough of first-aid to tell that he was mortally injured. Eileen had been flung over the balustrade of the bridge into the river far below. One of her shoes was caught between two stones on top of the bridge and helped to break her fall, but she was like Maurice in deep coma. Two doctors attended but there was little they could do. He was brought into Colbert's house nearby and neighbours prayed all night. Just as dawn brightened the sky he breathed his last. The memory of that terrible day will remain with me to my last breath. As I write these lines, the bitterness of that tragedy comes back to me with painful clarity. So full of life, so gay was he, in the prime of a life which gave great promise; suddenly he was snatched away from those he loved and who loved him. My Father was a broken man; my Mother, with her surpassing faith, accepted the blow, as she did many others, as God's Holy Will. My sister Joan, for whom Maurice had great affection, was wild with grief. Eileen was seriously ill for weeks but slowly recovered, though she bore the marks of her injuries for the rest of her life.

Before they left the house on that fatal day, Joan told Maurice that she had dreamt that he'd been in an accident. He laughed and told her not to be afraid.

With a heavy heart I set out for Dublin. The only one I confided in was my sister Mary Margaret, who was the soul of discretion. The reason I told her was that I knew she would kill herself worrying about me.

Kennedy had arranged a meeting for me with Austin Stack, a Kerryman then Minister for Home Affairs in the proscribed Dail. He turned up at the Clarence Hotel where I stayed. Curiously enough, his secret office was only a few yards away, as I was to discover soon. He was about fifty; a short, slightly-built fellow with a rather gnarled, pockmarked face and somewhat bitter expression. A polite man, he told me that Collins wanted to meet me and that arrangements would be made, but did not go any further into the matter. Joe O'Reilly* then arrived and fixed an appointment with Liam Tobin. I knew Joe's appearance well, indeed all the G-men did. He could be seen at all hours pedalling an old bicycle furiously. The G-men never attached any importance to Joe, but they were wrong. He was Collins' confidential courier and often carried important despatches. As Frank O'Connor said in his readable book, *The Big Fellow*, Joe lived only for Collins. Like him, he was a Corkman, a thin, eager, sparely-built youth with lively movements, a very dynamo of energy. He was also innocent, ingenuous and intensely religious; altogether an admirable person. A poor labourer, he had given up his work to take on a life of drudgery far worse than labouring, for Collins was a hard taskmaster, sparing none, himself least of all. Joe and I went to the Wicklow Hotel where we met Liam Tobin. Tall, gaunt, cynical, with tragic eyes, he looked a man who had seen the inside of hell. He walked without moving his arms and seemed emptied of energy. Yet this man was, after Collins, the Castle's most dangerous enemy. Like all of us, a poor man, an ex-shop assistant, he had a great flair for intelligence work, and was Collins' chief assistant. He ran a secret intelligence office within a stone's throw of the castle. It was never discovered

* O'Reilly served in the Civil Service in London with Collins and resigned to fight in the 1916 rebellion.

by the British. Untrained or self-trained as he was, he was an efficient counter-espionage agent and I believe would have been worth his place in any intelligence bureau. It is a measure of the G-men's impotence that they had not tagged Tobin though, as I shall show, the British secret service had. His motive in meeting me was to safeguard Collins and the revolutionary movement against a possible enemy, as many 'friends' had turned up sailing under false colours. By adroit questioning he sought to probe my mind, but as I had often withstood cross-examinations from my Father (who should have been at the Bar) following some escapade, I think Tobin was wasting his time. The result, however, must have been satisfactory as he arranged a meeting for me with Collins. Anyway, Collins was seeking me, not I him!

I will mention here two of the false friends in addition to Burns, referred to above. Bernard Hugh Mulloy was a red-cap, or military policeman or soldier clerk stationed in Dublin Castle. Of course this may not have been his true role as those fellows are like actors, playing many parts and possessing numerous cover stories. I imagine an ordinary red-cap would not display the form that Mulloy showed. He sought out Sinn Fein, especially Volunteer contacts, and offered to help in any way possible. He met Tobin and other prominent Volunteers who were on the run. Through some process not clear to me the Volunteers discovered that he was a wrong one and he was shot dead on the 25th of March 1920 by the squad in a Dublin street. G-men who searched his body showed me lists of S.F. suspects that he had written. There can be no doubt that he sought to entrap Collins and others. What the latter did not know, however, was that Mulloy had left a will in the castle, in which he stated that if he was shot, Liam Tobin was the man who would do it. That I learnt from another red-cap, a friend of Mulloy's, who told me he had often shadowed him when he went to meet Tobin. My informant was an Englishman with a rough, coarse face—my private name for him was Bulldog Drummond. I warned Tobin that this man was on the look-out for him and he lay low for a while, and a hunt began for my informant. The red-cap disappeared from the castle soon afterwards and I never saw him again. The will, of course, was handed over to the secret service and earned Tobin top place in the list of wanted men though no hint of these events reached the G-men. Curiously enough, Collins obtained the will years afterwards from U.S.A. There were at least three rival intelligence agencies employed by the British and as usual they were all jealous of one another. Another man resigned from the R.I.C., rejoined, and became an active enemy of the Volunteers. He was promoted rapidly. He formed a squad of policemen who had been fired at or otherwise ill-treated and they buzzed about Dublin in two Ford cars. They wore steel waistcoats and woe betide any Volunteer they laid eyes on. The Dublin Brigade lined the Northern quays one day in an effort to annihilate them, only to see them flying down the Southern quays. Next day they lined the latter but the Fords chased down the Northern quay. It took on the elements of a farce. In the event they escaped unscathed. A Volunteer named J. Conroy, waited outside the castle for them. When three of them emerged he shot them. It turned out though that they were three poor devils of dispatch riders in the R.I.C., one of them a brother of Detective Sergeant Hoey, shot earlier.

9

JOE O'REILLY brought me to an old three-storey Dublin house at the junction of Upper Abbey Street and Liffey Street, then an unfrequented place. It was owned by two brothers named Bannon and was never raided by the British. It is no longer a public-house. O'Reilly knocked at the hall-door which gave entry to the owners' rooms. It was opened immediately by one of them. He was a good-looking man of about forty, a quiet-spoken fellow. He led us up the narrow stairs to a smoking-room with parlour chairs, a big table, a mantlepiece with a stuffed pheasant. It was a gloomy place and smelled of stale beer and bad air.

A tall, handsome man of about thirty who was alone rose from his chair and greeted us. This was my first glimpse of the famed Michael Collins. He was about six feet tall. Sturdily built, athletic, broad-shouldered, with a winning smile, a ready laugh and cheerful manner. He had a trick of turning his head swiftly and then the resolute line of his jaw showed. He was a friendly man with the fortunate manners of putting one at ease. He was dressed in an ill-fitting tweed suit which had cycling clips on the pants. An old soft hat and a cheap dust-coat were thrown on a chair. Shaking my hand with a firm grip, he said: 'I know you and your brothers are all right (i.e. friendly to the revolution)—it is too bad about Moss's death. You shouldn't have been let resign—there was a misunderstanding. I want you to go back to the castle to work for us.' 'Mr Collins,' I said, 'there's nothing I should hate more than to go back there; I'll do anything else for you; join a flying column or anything.' 'Listen, Dave,' he said, 'we have plenty of men for columns, but on the other hand no one can fill your place in the castle, for they trust you and we trust you.' Only the two of us were present at this conversation. After some further talk I agreed to go back. I told Collins that some days would elapse before it was known whether I'd be successful. We parted, and I wrote to the Commissioner of the D.M. Police applying to rejoin. A G-man named Lynch turned up next day with the reply. The Commissioner's Secretary asked me to call at his office next day. I duly went to the castle and was ushered into the Commissioner's office. Colonel Johnston greeted me in a kindly manner. Even today I am ashamed at deceiving him, so charming a person was he. He asked me why I desired to rejoin. I produced the threatening letters, which he read.

He questioned me about conditions in the country and I told him the truth, which was unpalatable to him. Of course he knew the state of affairs himself, better than I did. He told me I could have any station I chose, decently enough. I replied that the G Division would suit me. He agreed. It was said that Colonel Johnston took his orders from the Kildare Street Club—a landlord and unionist coterie then wielding great influence with the British. That may well have been true. After all, if he had not been the right colour he would not have got the job. For, let there be no error, religious and racial discrimination was rife in that regime. A Catholic could not, as a general rule, rise beyond a few steps in both police forces, though that attitude was modified under the stress of war. The most amusing thing about the upper echelons of the R.I.C. was their social status-seeking. Most county inspectors were social climbers, ornamental rather than of use. A double-barrelled name and membership of the Masons and Kildare Street Club were hallmarks. At this time the R.I.C. was headed by an ex-British army officer named Byrne, but he did not prove warlike enough for the administration, so they fired him and appointed an Orangeman named Smith whom I was to meet in dramatic circumstances. Over him and heading the Auxiliaries and Black & Tans, sat General Tudor, a protégé of Churchill's. A brother of our school inspector, Right Hon. James McMahon, was Under-Secretary at the castle. He was said to be a protégé of Cardinal Logue. He wielded no real power. That was in the hands of his colleagues Sir John Anderson and Mr Cope. Anderson was a Scot, Cope an Englishman and protégé of

Lloyd George. I never met Tudor nor Anderson, though Cope and I met three times. Discrimination held sway in the G Division too. A Mohammedan, Jew, Turk, Orangeman or Armenian had a better chance of promotion than an Irish Catholic. Personally, of course, I, a junior, had no grievance on that score, but am describing the scene as it appeared to me. Back I went to report to Bruton, now a chief inspector in charge of the political wing of the G Division stationed in Dublin Castle. He looked at me with quizzical glance. 'Oh! So you came back to us? How did they treat you in the country?' The threatening letters did duty again. He read them. 'You were wise to clear out.' He detailed me to escort the Recorder of Dublin, familiarly known to one and all as Tommy Shaughnessy.

Somehow, I had an uneasy feeling that shrewd old Bruton was not altogether taken in by my story. At the back of his mind perhaps was a suspicion that all was not lovely in the garden. But he probably dismissed such thoughts as groundless and he was always friendly to me. There was another Tipperary man in the unit who had great influence with him. He and I were close friends though of course he, too, did not know of my dual role. Still he probably vouched for me with Bruton. The Recorder (a judge of quarter-sessions), a man then of about sixty, was short in stature. He had a white face and a flowing mane of white hair like Lloyd George. A lively little man, he was a confirmed snuff-taker like a lot of old-fashioned lawyers. His cravat and the front of his coat were covered and discoloured with it. Tommy was a privy councillor, and perhaps it was this that rated him an escort from the castle. Another member of H.M. Privy Council, Mr Brooks, a railway director, had been shot by the Volunteers in Dublin a short time earlier. It was said that he advocated bringing over English railwaymen as the locals refused to cart British troops and Tans about.* According to *Chambers's Encyclopaedia*, a privy councillor's duties are 'defined by the oath to advise the King (or the Viceroy) to the best of his cunning and discretion. Membership is a coveted honour, conferring rank (of Right Honourable), precedence and titular dignity.' I am not so sure that the rank was coveted in Dublin *circa* 1920, especially after Brooks was shot.

* 2,000 were sacked for refusing to man troop trains.

76

This business of having an escort was a two-edged weapon, even if the escort meant business! While an escort probably would not save the escortee from being shot, it had the disadvantage of pointing the finger at the person being escorted. This was proved in the case of Alan Bell. Though Collins maintained an efficient intelligence service, it had blind spots like all such machines. It knew nothing of Mr Bell nor of his activities. He was an ex-stipendiary, i.e. a paid magistrate, whose title in Ireland was Resident Magistrate. Curiously enough he was also an ex-district inspector of the R.I.C. Apparently a versatile fellow, he was now engaged in secret and lethal employment, to wit, investigating Sinn Fein funds. At this time, Collins was Minister for Finance in the proscribed Dail or Sinn Fein Parliament, as well as Director of Intelligence in the Volunteers, or rebel army. A Dail Loan had been launched to provide the sinews of war. Several millions had been scraped up at home and abroad, notably from Irish immigrants in U.S.A. Collins, of course, could not lodge this vital money in any bank account. The British, with their excellent lines in those establishments, could poke out and grab it. There were no Sinn Fein bank managers! So what he did was to lodge some of that money in the names of some rich sympathisers. This is what Bell was after.

He set up a kind of Star Chamber in the Castle. In March 1920, he was given power, under an ancient statute known as the Crimes Act, to send for and interrogate bank managers and others in order to lay hands on that money. It is thought that he carried out similar enquiries into Parnell's funds. He lived beyond the Dalkey tramline and was escorted by R.I.C. men to that tram every morning, and met at the Dublin end by G-men. One of the latter told me who he was and what he was doing. At my meeting with Kennedy in Tralee I told him what I knew about Bell and suggested that he should be investigated. Soon afterwards, in May, Bell was shot at Merrion. No one filled his place. The fact that he had an escort, and one which stupidly gave him no protection on his journey, directed attention to him. At the same time, of course, a day would have come when his activities came to Collins' notice and then he was doomed. Collins was not the man to allow this war-chest which had been so painfully gathered to be taken from under his nose. Actually, what I did say to Kennedy was that it was a hellish mistake to shoot poor devils of police who were at the bottom of the ladder. Though the British then and later made every effort to smash and grab that Loan, they did not succeed. A certain amount of it, in gold, was buried under a concrete floor in Batt O'Connor's house in Donnybrook. It remained there undisturbed until the war was over. The British offered £5,000 reward for the capture of Bell's killers but to no avail.

I met Sergeants Broy and Kavanagh and Detective McNamara on a new footing. Broy and Kavanagh were stationed in Brunswick Street and were clerks in the detective office there. Often I had sensed that they were no friends of the regime; now I learnt that they had been working secretly for Collins, Kavanagh since 1916 or 1917. Kavanagh was the eldest of the three. He was about sixty years old, a neatly made, short, dapper little Dublin man with waxed moustache. He was good-humoured, witty. When the old Superintendent 'Butt' Brien used to come into the office of a morning, Kavanagh used to say: 'Get your faces ready for the Superintendent's joke, boys.' Alas! Kavanagh was soon to die in hospital, of heart failure, mourned by all who knew him. Broy was about twenty-six, broad-faced, rather stooped, an enigmatic character. A native of Kildare, he had only one love, athletics, and one hate, the British Empire. As he was an official typist, he made an extra carbon copy of every confidential report for Collins. Collins stored up these—and when they were found—stored up trouble for Broy. McNamara, a lithe, smart Dublin-born son of a police officer, was at that time a confidential clerk for the Assistant Commissioner in the castle and was, I think, a relative of Kavanagh. He was a charming fellow, light-hearted and great fun. Like all soccer players he was nimble-footed and when walking along the street, would trip one up. One night, he and I were having a drink with a hotelier, when he started fishing tumblers out of my pocket, accusing me of robbing the place. Of course, our host knew Mac's tricks.

When the G Division split and the political branch moved to the Castle, Broy and Kavanagh were left out on a limb. That is why Collins wanted me to go back there. Broy, McNamara and myself used to meet Collins once a week in the house of Tommy

78

Gay, 8 Haddon Road, Clontarf. This was a quiet, suburban place, several miles from the city. Gay, a tiny Dublin man, with bronchial trouble which made his life a burden, was librarian in Capel Street Municipal Library. Like nearly all the *dramatis personae* of the revolution, he led a double life; a bookworm openly and also, secretly, a confidential courier for Collins. He was so unobtrusive that neither the library nor his home ever came under suspicion. He and his charming wife were the soul of discretion. Such people were a Godsend to Collins. I often left urgent messages in the library and one could be sure of their prompt and safe delivery. As I pushed my way through a lot of down and outs who frequented the reading-room, it used to strike me that the place would be the last to be suspected by the British, and I was right. The three of us G-men travelled separately on trams to Gay's house. Collins generally cycled on an ancient machine. I shall not soon forget the terror on poor Mrs Gay's face when she answered my ring. Every time that bell went she was sure it was the enemy. This strain, I am sure, shortened her life. She was a lovely and charming hostess, and used to give us tea and home-made pancakes that Collins loved. She and I were great friends and I still look back with affection to those days when, in spite of her fears, she welcomed us. And her fears were no idle fears, burdened as she was by a young and helpless family. When she heard I was escorting Tommy Shaughnessy she laughed and said, 'And that's my maiden name too.'

Tobin brought Rory O'Connor along to a meeting in Bannon's pub. They were close friends and Rory often came there with us. One day when an old G-man and I passed through St Stephen's Green, a city park, my colleague indicated Rory sitting on a bench. 'See him, Dave? He is a prominent Sinn Feiner; if he is there tomorrow we'll have him pulled in.' I warned Tobin and Rory came along to thank me. He was a man of middle age, short, very thin, with haggard pale face, and a deep voice. He was good company, a great talker, very cheerful. We became close friends. Employed by Dublin Corporation, he was at this time Director of Engineering of G.H.Q. in the secret army of the I.R.A. or Volunteers.

The Bannons of the pub got frightened and told us not to come any more. We met mostly in the street after that. We did not blame the publicans as no one wants to meet sudden death if he can avoid it. They were out only to make money. There was a very quiet place in the city outside Jervis Street Hospital, and there I often met my contacts. Collins, Tobin and Cullen often came to the Wicklow Hotel for lunch. Paddy O'Shea, a Kerry waiter, was a trusted man and often served me with a despatch under the soup plate. It was known, though, that the hall-porter was an informer, and he was shot. One night, the three of us G-men met Collins as usual in Gay's house. As he was in a hurry that night, a taxi driven by trusted Joe Hyland called for him. He offered us a lift into the city, which we accepted. We had only gone a half-mile when we were held up by a squad of Tommies across the road. Collins jumped out, suspecting a trap, but we persuaded him to come back in. An English officer came over and asked us who we were. We answered that we were detectives looking for Collins.

He said, 'By Jove, that explains it! Those blighters were waiting for you. They've just thrown a bomb at us! If I were you I'd go back and return some other way.' We thanked him, Joe wheeled the old taxi about and we cleared off. Hyland and his old wagon went right through the whole war without ever being suspected. His brother Batty was used also with the same result. They were cheerful fellows who faced danger and difficulty with unconcern.

A character in one of O'Casey's plays which deals with the revolution says: 'Kathleen ni Houlihan [the symbolical figure of Ireland] was always a saint, but be God she's a raging divil now.' So far as the British were concerned she certainly was, in those days!

The Dublin police, apart from the G-men, were very careful not to stick their necks out and escaped practically unscathed. The R.I.C., though, were in the thick of it and were boycotted. A lot of them resigned, some under duress, but those who remained had a very tough time, plenty of them being ambushed and killed. Ishmaels, they had every man's hand against them. Sinn Fein blundered where the R.I.C. was concerned. Many of those poor devils were married with families, generally large ones, and had

80

no resources apart from their pay. A vigorous propaganda was directed at them with the object of making them resign, but no effort was made by anybody to provide alternative employment or to help them to return to civilian life. The result was that they could see nothing ahead but starvation. So literally they stuck to their guns and fought their own countrymen—to the last. I am well aware that our war-chest was far from overflowing in those days, but some effort, even to pay their fares abroad, should have been made. Instead, that terrible weapon, the boycott, immensely cruel, was used against them. No one would speak to them or to their wives or children, shopkeepers would not serve them, nor undertakers bury them. Naturally such treatment filled them with hatred and bitterness. They acted as the eyes and ears of the Black and Tans and fought strenuously for their British masters. So bitter was the hatred they engendered, that after the struggle the survivors had to leave the country until time produced other victims.

However, that is not to say that they were all hostile to Sinn Fein. Many R.I.C. men helped actively and others turned a blind eye to the rebels. To my own knowledge, one county inspector, two or three district inspectors and countless sergeants and privates rendered the movement useful service, now lost in the mists of history. Drawn from a good class of people and marrying their own sort, they suddenly found themselves in a terrible jam with a revolution going full blast. It is impossible to withhold some sympathy from those men in this terrible predicament. God alone knows how they suffered.

Times of unrest are always difficult for police and of course anyone who stands in the road of revolution is bound to get the wrong end of the stick. Contrary to what is thought generally, the Irish are a peaceable people, but when roused they can be ruthless.

10

EVERY G-man kept a diary in the office wherein he
entered particulars of his day's activities. This generally consisted
of names of suspects he had seen, or maybe the comings and
goings at some place under observation. The suspects the G-men
noted were generally 'oul cods' who were quite harmless, and
had long ago lost their revolutionary ardour, if such they'd ever
had. The G-men did not know that a new group of activists had
taken over. They were short of informers. These creatures of the
dark had ever been the Castle's last line of defence. In every age
an Irish Judas was hidden in the undergrowth. All of them posed
as ultra-patriotic; some were *agents provocateurs*. Others were
attorneys who 'defended' leading rebels, secretly betraying them.
One was the Attorney 'defending' Robert Emmet, whom he
helped to execution in 1803.

During the First World War and prior to the rebellion of 1916,
the British were kept fully posted as to the liaison between Irish
rebels such as John Devoy in U.S.A. and the German Government. The Irish hoped to obtain arms from the Germans. In the
office of Von Bernstorff, German Minister in Washington,
worked a cipher-clerk. He was a Czech patriot, probably recruited
for the British by Benês, their leader. This man leaked all confidential messages he could lay hands on to Captain Guy Gaunt,
British Naval Attaché in that city. This accounts for the arms
ship *Aud* being seized by H.M. Navy and many other occurrences
mysterious at the time. I've read reams of highly coloured
accounts of the successes of Admiral 'Blinker' Hall in breaking
German ciphers and doubtless there was some truth in it, but the
Czech is never mentioned. The irony of his activities is that he

82

has not improved his country's status, they having exchanged whips for scorpions. The point I am making is that the British were very often lucky enough to have their man in the right place. They are, of course, most careful not to expose him. This was a lesson Collins was slow to learn, as will be apparent later. Espionage is one of the toughest games played. An agent in the right place is hard to find, but when he is found he should be regarded as a pearl beyond price, like a good wife! Everything should be let go by the board rather than that he should be exposed. There are basic laws in that game and that is the first one.

II

W HEN the G-men were decimated and rendered
nearly harmless and the R.I.C. driven in from their outposts at
the cross-roads, so depriving their masters of an intelligence service
in the countryside, the British faced a serious situation. Yet not
one unfamiliar to them. That is the best of having an empire;
you get plenty of experience in putting down rebellions! In some
corner of it trouble is bound to be found and the pattern differs,
but only in detail. Consequently, they are nearly always ready for
a dust-up, though they pretend otherwise. They are a people who
do not give up easily, as their enemies have found to their cost.

Any other nation would have thrown in the sponge at the time
of Haig's 'offensives' in the First War when the British Army
incurred casualties of fifty or sixty thousand in one day. Any other
army would have mutinied, as the French did, and would have
been justified, but the poor British Tommy still blindly obeyed
the man with one stripe, the lance-corporal.

In 1918 the British had emerged victorious from the most
gruelling struggle in their long history. So they were not disposed
to surrender Ireland to a handful of revolutionaries, badly armed
and only partially supported by the populace. Instead, they
flooded Ireland with reinforcements, to wit, hundreds of conscript troops, Black and Tans, Auxiliaries, and hundreds of secret
agents. The Black and Tans and the Auxiliaries were new entities.
I shall try to describe them briefly. They both arrived in Ireland
in March 1920.

It was clear to the British that the R.I.C. was in its depleted
and demoralised state practically finished, like the G Division; so
they decided to augment it. Recruits could not be found in

84

Ireland. So recruiting posters went up at every Unemployment Exchange in Great Britain, asking for recruits to fill vacancies in the R.I.C. Of course they did not tell how the vacancies had arisen! Potential recruits had no information as to conditions in Ireland except that provided by their newspapers. As these, to a great extent, were owned by lords and dukes who could not be described exactly as pro-Irish, the presentation of such news was bound to be one-sided. From what the lords told them, those poor devils may have imagined that they were going on a crusade for England, Home and Beauty. One a lot nearer home than jousting with the Turks.

So thousands of them joined the Black and Tans at about £5 per week. The R.I.C. stores had not enough uniforms for them, so they were dressed partly in khaki and partly in R.I.C. bottle-blue. They therefore appeared in this motley ensemble which truly suited their character, for they were neither soldiers nor policemen. A well-known pack of hounds in Tipperary is called the Black and Tans (this being the colour of the animals) and some wit so christened the new force. The name stuck. It was not to be the last time a police irregular outfit in Ireland bore the name of a hunting pack. Twelve thousand Tans were recruited. It is no exaggeration to say that the country was flooded with them. They had a great encampment at Gormanstown, Co. Meath, and the R.I.C. Depot, Phoenix Park, Dublin was a staging area. Being ex-soldiers they were, of course, familiar with infantry weapons: rifles, revolvers, grenades and machine-guns. They were well supplied with all of those. They had plenty of transport consisting of army lorries and fast tenders. Their drivers were regular dare-devils. Parties of Tans were sent as reinforcements to each R.I.C. barrack. They proceeded to create a regular reign of terror wherever they went. And worst of all, the hard core of R.I.C. who remained in the force, embittered by the palpable hate surrounding them, acted as their eyes and ears and paid off many old scores. The Tans, of course, being strangers, were not in a position to know who was who. Many Volunteers and sympathisers were assassinated. The Tans made no pretence to be policemen; they were an irregular military force, had no discipline and were guilty of terrible outrages against the people and mostly against non-combatants.

They stole everything they could lay hands on, like those Free Companies that roamed through France long ago; burning, shooting and robbing. It was said that many of them were ex-convicts. It would not be the first time that jail gates opened in a crisis. Arthur Bryant in his readable book, *The Age of Chivalry* (Collins 1963), tells us (p. 265) of a band of robbers in Sherwood forest who had robbed and murdered a Judge and . . . were pardoned in return for service with the Royal Army in Scotland *circa* 1345. The Tans brought their women with them. When the lorries were about to leave on their daily raiding sorties, those females used to shout: 'George, four jolly heads today.' This meant a raid on some fowl-house.

As I have mentioned, the Depot, Phoenix Park was their H.Q. It is a huge pile with a large square in front. One day Lord French, the unsuccessful cavalry general of the First War who was Lord Lieutenant of Ireland was vacating that office. It was said he would address the R.I.C. and Tans at the Depot. I went along to see the fun. There was an immense parade of those fellows. Old French, a pot-bellied little man with fierce moustache, attacked the Sinn Feiners, whom he called poisonous insects. After his speech, the R.I.C. band, a very good outfit, struck up 'I'm forever blowing bubbles'—a perfect commentary. Just as, at Yorktown when a British Army surrendered to the embattled U.S. farmers, their band rendered 'The World turned upside down'. Band-masters must possess a peculiar sense of humour.

Most people confuse the Black and Tans with the Auxiliaries, but they were distinct forces. The Auxiliaries started off with some pretence to be a *corps d'élite*. They were a brain-child of Churchill's, who got the idea from the Boer War, and from his one-time ally, the White Russian Army. This had formations consisting solely of ex-officers, for the very good reason that a great majority of their military officers were then anti-red. The Auxies, as they came to be called, were originally called Temporary Cadets and bore the letters T.C.* on their shoulder-straps. This was a pretence that they would eventually become officers in the R.I.C. which their masters held out as bait for recruits. Churchill also chose their leader, General Tudor who, he says in one of his

* The Auxiliaries' own interpretation of those letters is unprintable.

86

books, impressed him in France during the First War. The Auxies were all ex-officers and came from all quarters of the globe. I met ex-cowboys from U.S.A. and Canada, trappers from Alaska, Scots, South Africans, and two Jews. Most were English and Scots. They were organised in fifteen companies and had at their head Brigadier-General Crozier, late of the British Army. He resigned in disgust when Tudor (who was Chief of all the Police) would not back him up in enforcing discipline. If anyone wants to pursue the short history of the Auxies he should read Crozier's book, *Ireland for Ever!*, which can be found in any library.

An Auxie company consisted of about sixty or seventy men, with section leaders and a commanding officer. Their H.Q. in Dublin was at Beggars Bush Barracks. They had F Company at the castle, with others at the North Wall and others in the provinces: two or four in Cork, one company at North Dublin Union. They were hefty young fellows, neatly dressed with some pride in their appearance. Generally they wore khaki tunics belonging to their army service complete with decorations, military riding breeches and a Glengarry woolly cap. I have no idea how they came to wear this curious headgear. I suppose some quartermaster discovered a dump of them in some store or perhaps bought them via a good rake-off from the wholesaler. I had a good view of F Company in the castle and got to know them and their leaders. They were a thoroughly dangerous mob and far more intelligent than the Tans. Several of them told me frankly that they joined because they had no job and no prospect and were disgusted with their present role. It is perfectly true that thousands of British ex-officers were demobbed after the war and found themselves down and out. In this situation they were ready to take on any job with pay.

Each Auxie carried two heavy (·45) Webley revolvers strapped to his thighs, cowboy fashion, a rifle, with pouches and bandolier full of ammunition. Their transport consisted of fast Crossley tenders in which they sat in two rows back to back. Their drivers were even more reckless than those of the Tans! Sometimes they carried civilian hostages such as Sean O'hUadhaig, a Sinn Fein solicitor. At their disposal were armoured cars powered by Rolls Royce engines and armed with one or two revolving turrets firing

Vickers machine-guns. These vehicles were formidable weapons of war and very fast. Their pay, too was at a higher rate than that of the Tans, being £1 per day. A lot of this went on liquor as they had a wet canteen in each company. I saw, night after night, their C.O. in a Dublin barracks (not the castle) being frog-marched to a Crossley tender by two section-leaders. He was so drunk that the only thing he could say was that he wanted to 'have a crack at the Shinners'. He wore a khaki tunic with a brigadier's insignia. When sober, he was quite a decent sort of fellow. It was pitiful to see the demoralisation of a human being in that *milieu*. Crozier I've never seen, but he may have been a good type of officer.

The castle presented a lively scene every night. Lorry engines racing made the night hideous, searchlights were being tested, rolls of barbed wire assembled. The Auxies and Tommies regularly fenced in city blocks and searched every building inside.

Collins had an ancient bicycle whose chain rattled like a mediaeval ghost's. One very foggy night as I walked along Nassau Street I heard its characteristic sound and said to myself, 'That's Collins' old bike.' I stood out on the middle of the street as he pedalled furiously towards me. 'I've just left Parnell Square,' he laughed. 'There's hordes of Tommies and Auxies up there wiring in the whole place.'

Occasionally I visited the Auxies' canteen with McNamara. Their quarters were just inside the castle lower gate. The place was known as Exchange Court. They were hard drinkers and drank all hard liquor. Gin, whiskey and brandy consumed most of their pay.

They had numerous so-called intelligence officers, but these were really terrorists, most wore steel waistcoats, and one definitely had a slate off. Another pretended that he had been wounded and applied to the Recorder's Court under the Malicious Injuries Act, receiving a substantial reward. Under this statute, millions of Irish money were paid out to adherents of the British. It really amounted to collective fines on the population. A number of these claims like the one mentioned here, were faked and supported by perjury.

The Auxies caught two youths on the night of 9th February

1921 in Dublin. They had rebel ballads in their pockets but were not in the Volunteers or Fianna boy-scouts. Their dead bodies were found next morning at an outlying place. Another night an Auxie who was of giant stature murdered a woman with a bayonet outside the castle. Needless to say these crimes went undetected and unpunished. Two Auxies with their English girl friends went into Pim's stores one day which is quite near the castle. Those females chose two of the most expensive fur coats in the place. When the shopman produced the bill, the Auxies drew their guns and all walked out.

Yet the picture was not all black. Several Auxies turned up at a courtmartial on S. McKeon, an I.R.A. column man and gave evidence in his favour. In another case known to me, his comrades reimbursed a man swindled by one of them.

It must be said that the Dublin Brigade did not inflict many casualties on the Auxies. A few were shot in Grafton Street by the Active Service Unit. There was an exchange of firing at their H.Q. at the North Wall, but this was only a minor affair. No serious attack was made on them. Because of their mobility, good armaments and irregular movements, together with their readiness for a fight, they presented a very difficult target. Added to this, of course, was the fact that the Dublin Brigade was wretchedly armed. I doubt if they possessed even one machine-gun, let alone any kind of artillery or mortar, or if they did, they were under wraps.

The British kept a tank in the castle. As I watched once, I saw it knock down a tall stone wall in an effort to turn. It used to waddle about the city regularly presumably in an effort to over-awe the wild Irish. It was said that Jimmy Conroy, the one-man column who shot the despatch riders, 'attacked' it with a ·38 revolver. An old apple-woman remarked as it trundled by: 'Begod! Butt Bridge going for a walk!' This Liffey Bridge, on account of its oval girders, looks like a huge tank, right enough.

The British had enormous garrisons in Dublin, which was ringed about with military barracks containing hundreds of men, well armed and very mobile, so that anyone shooting up the Auxies would have to anticipate massive reinforcements hurriedly coming to their aid.

The Volunteers were really only a part-time army. Nearly all of them were working men, so that their only free time was at night or early in the morning. British Military G.H.Q. was at Parkgate and had dozens of civilian clerks. Many of these were secretly members of the Volunteer or I.R.A. movement. One, with whom I was acquainted, was a tiny fellow named Sean Tumbleton who regularly bombed the Tommies at a narrow street called Redmond's Hill and Camden Street, which consequently the Tommies called the Dardanelles. Tumbleton was a company captain and when a vacancy occurred in British G.H.Q. he recommended his Volunteer adjutant, an even tinier midget called Martin Hoare. The latter was arrested while armed so Tumbleton had to go on the run. One of my funniest recollections is (years later) of Hoare dressed up in the uniform of a policeman which was made for a 6 foot 3 inch giant. The helmet rested on his shoulders and the top-coat had a train behind like an evening frock. The chin-strap of the helmet beat on his microscopic chest. He was a decent, loyal little fellow and so was Tumbleton.

The Auxies, too, accomplished very little and scarcely made a dent in the Volunteers, with the exception of their slaughter of Dick McKee, the O.C. of the Dublin Brigade. This I shall describe later. It was well known that they used to torture and terrorize prisoners. Anyone who fell into their hands was nearly certain to be in for a bad time. Many a man had his teeth knocked out and was savagely ill-treated. Of course some prisoners talked to save themselves, and who could blame them?

As well, they had touts working outside for them; poor wretches who were on the look-out for easy money. A strict curfew was maintained by the British in Dublin and elsewhere. What purpose this primitive device served always puzzled me, unless it was indeed a kind of collective punishment for the citizens. If its purpose was to hamper revolutionary activities, then it can be said that it was a total failure, just as the trundling tank was a waste of good fuel.

General Tudor, the Chief of Police, wisely took no chances travelling about: he was always in an armoured car. General McCready was Commander of the troops in Ireland, and he too did not present a target. He was the son of the famous Shakesperian actor. His grandfather was a poor Dublin upholsterer who emigrated to London long ago. The General, who served in the First War, then became Commissioner of the London Police. The Welsh miners in a village called Tonypandy rioted. Lloyd George sent McCready to 'restore order', which he did. The Welsh wizard thereupon concluded that he was the right man to subdue the Paddies, but I'm afraid he bit off more than he could chew. He was a rough-looking fellow with a cauliflower ear.

An officer in the Auxiliaries offered his services to Collins as an agent and asked that someone should meet him. This dangerous assignment was filled by Frank Thornton and Bob O'Neill, two of Collins' intelligence men. The man promised to work for the rebels if he was paid and is said to have given valuable information. Later he was transferred to the country and figured in a mysterious affair with some Volunteers, which resulted in their arrest. This was after the Truce. I knew the man well. He was an ex-physical instructor and of hefty build. He disappeared after the show was over. One of the Volunteers, Jim Hannon, shot his way out of a similar tight corner when surrounded by Auxies.

As I have said, when the G-men were more or less demoralised, the British flooded the place with secret-service men. Some of these were civilians, some serving British officers, some ex-officers and N.C.O.s and some professional agents. Most were Anglo-Irish or British, though their head, Count Sévigné, may have been French and looked it. Of course those fellows had a different name and cover story for every day of the week, so unless one knew one from birth, one could not be sure of his identity. I am told that the first intimation the relatives of some had of their occupation was when their dead bodies were sent home. As my story unfolds I shall deal further with those mysterious men, of whom so little is known.

Sergeant Broy and I pretended to be mutually hostile and this was a wise precaution as things turned out. He was now a pay sergeant in Brunswick Street, having been promoted into poor Kavanagh's post. He worked in the Superintendent's office where I often called for an exchange of notes. Needless to say it was not the defence of the realm that concerned us.

He was generally alone in the room but sometimes the Superintendent used to burst in. His name was J. J. Purcell and he had recently been promoted from the uniform force where he had perhaps thirty years' service. With his ramrod back, closely-cut hair, rimless glasses, gruff voice and solemn face, he looked like a caricature of a Prussian officer. He loathed G-men. The first thing he did when he was promoted was to hold an unofficial press conference (a thing unheard of in the police then). He told the newsmen that he had been transferred to the G Division against his will, that he would concern himself solely with non-political matters; in fact he made it abundantly clear that he was going to sit out this war. This was pretty steep for a member of a disciplined force, but though the Castle fumed, they did nothing except to send Sergeant Beggs to watch him. That is surely a measure of their bewilderment at the time. So the last thing J. J. Purcell wanted to see in his private office was a member of the political police. He made this clear, too, glaring at me as I smilingly made for the door. His language was pretty uninhibited, like mine at times. Broy used to tell me of the dialogue following my visits, which never varied:

P. 'What in the name of . . . brings that fellow here?'

B. 'Looking for more money! Thinks he's entitled to some other allowance. Says he's not getting paid enough!'

P. 'James' St! What's the job coming to? When I was a young man I was afraid to even look at the Superintendent, never mind coming into his office. Warn him to keep out of here! Blast them! Maybe that pimp Bruton is sending him here spying on us? You couldn't tell what those fellows are up to! They'll get us all shot, damn and blast them!'

B. 'I don't think so. He's simply looking for more cash.'

P. 'Damn him. It's too well paid they are. I can't stand them!'
This farce went on for a long time. The poor sap to the day of his death firmly believed that I was trying to draw water from the rock. Actually he was not a bad fellow. Though he could curse like a trooper he had a rooted objection to such language from his subordinates. Once he was heard to shout at them: 'The next bloody man I hear using such language will be brought before the (unprintable) Commissioner.' Later, I was told that he had a 'you

92

don't scratch me and I don't scratch you' arrangement with the local Volunteers. Certainly he provided us with a little light relief at the time.

The old G-men, in order to demonstrate their loyalty to the Crown, subscribed for a huge portrait of Queen Victoria which had a heavy gilt frame. Hung in a prominent place in the mess-room, her homely mug was the first thing to be seen on entering. Broy and I often discussed bumping it off. One drowsy summer afternoon an old inspector named Redmond was on duty in the public office while an Orangeman, a sergeant, dozed on a sofa under the portrait. These two were mutually hostile. Broy rushed down the stairs and fired several shots from a tiny pistol at the Queen's picture and flew up again. Redmond, hearing the noise, rushed in to find the Sergeant covered with glass and frame. He immediately accused the Sergeant of breaking up the picture and of course this was a mortal insult to a man from the Black Chapter. A hellish row ensued, but we saw Victoria no more.

Often I was sent on duty with an elderly detective inspector and detective sergeant. They were supposed to be investigating the killing of Barton, Smyth and Hoey. They spent each day on a pub-crawl and did no investigating as they wanted to stay alive. They drank steadily from 10 a.m. until 6 p.m.—all whiskey—with an interval for lunch. I was then a teetotaller and my tipple was lemonade. They used to explain to the publicans that I was not a miser, such being the usual label for a non-drinker. At evening-time I felt like a poisoned pup after those soft drinks. Thank God I've never touched them since! Those two used to get very drunk. As one was newly married I had to see him home often. Someone told me that fish and chips had a sobering effect, like black coffee is said to have, so every evening I went into a little shop and bought two packets. I can't say though that the prescription showed any sign of being effective. I often pitied the new wife, whom I never saw, parting with her husband outside their door.

Regularly they had to submit reports on the progress of their 'investigation'. This task they had to face in the morning when their heads were jumping off. So they used to call on me to help and lend colour to an otherwise bald and unconvincing narrative.

I cannot now recall the deathless prose we used, but I recollect the last sentence which ran: 'Every effort will be made to apprehend the perpetrators of this dastardly outrage.' The Castle had to be satisfied with this Johnsonian pearl and that is as far as they got.

Those two old men were charming fellows. Surprisingly enough they did not die of cirrhosis of the liver—I imagine theirs were made of corrugated iron. They lived to a good age and were pensioned.

Broy warned me that a couple of the Orangemen in the place were hostile to me, but I took no notice of them. Neither did anybody else. They were in an abject state of fright and hardly ever left the castle, especially after one (the better of them) was shot and wounded.

In order to try to retain their grip on the provinces, the British decentralised their control of the R.I.C. and Tans by appointing Divisional Commissioners of the R.I.C. One of these, a Colonel Smyth was D.C. of Cork and Kerry. He visited the Listowel R.I.C. Barracks on 18th June 1920 where he harangued the party of five or six. He told them that the more Sinn Feiners they shot, the better he would be pleased. One of the R.I.C. named Mee replied: 'Sir, by your accent you come from England, but in your ignorance you forget you are speaking to Irishmen.' Thereupon all the party threw down their belts and resigned from the force. One, a man named Hughes afterwards became a priest and was made a bishop later. Another was Sheeran who still lives. An R.I.C. man named O'Connell who served in Killarney wrote an account of the affair to a friar of his acquaintance. The letter was seized by the Tans and O'Connell was dismissed. His brother, Inspector E. M. O'Connell, was later my confidential clerk and faithful friend for many years. Cosgrave's government afterwards rewarded those men with pensions but at the time they were left to fend for themselves. This bears out my contention that Sinn Fein acted towards the R.I.C. in a very short-sighted manner. Divisional Commissioner Smyth was shot dead in a Cork hotel some days later. His brother was shot by Breen and Treacy in the episode at Professor Carolan's house in Dublin.

The Friar to whom O'Connell wrote was beaten up and imprisoned by the Auxies. The late Catholic Bishop of Cork prohibited his clergy from giving the Last Sacraments to condemned I.R.A. men but the Capuchins defied him and attended those poor wretches. After the Truce two of them, Friars Albert and Dominic, were exiled to U.S.A. and died there. Their bodies were brought home to lie in Irish earth, in Rochestown Co. Cork.

Discussing the matter with a distinguished Churchman I told him: the Bishop was right; he was going by the Book: we broke every law, Human and Divine.

Though it is outside the scope of this book, perhaps I shall be forgiven for saying something about the attitude of the Catholic Church in Ireland towards the revolution. About ninety per cent of the Irish people are Catholics, ninety-three in the territory of the Republic. They have clung to that faith through ages despite dungeon, fire and sword. It would be hard to find in the world any people more devoted to Catholicism. Most of the hierarchy, that is to say the cardinal, archbishops and bishops were neutral in the struggle, so were the senior clergy. There are many reasons for this. A priest, as a rule is a man of peace. All his training and instincts are against violence and towards the rule of law. The Church had been persecuted since the Reformation and draconian laws operated against it.

Following on Daniel O'Connell's agitation, Wellington and Peel carried the R.C. Relief Bill in 1829, which provided, *inter alia*, freedom of worship. Yet, up to recent times, the British Government had a say at the Vatican on the appointment of Irish bishops. The Church has a long memory. It had seen risings, revolts, dynamiters, plans of campaign, all failing, with resultant dire punishment for those involved. So it feared Sinn Fein would go the same road. There was also, of course, a question of Moral Law involved.

The younger clergy were openly or covertly sympathisers with Sinn Fein. One, Fr Griffin of Galway, was lured from his home at night by British forces (Auxiliaries) on the pretext that he was wanted to give the last sacraments to a dying parishioner. His dead body was found in a bog. Canon Magner, a harmless old man of over seventy, was shot dead by Auxies on a Cork road in

95

daylight. Dr Fogarty, Bishop of Killaloe, an ardent sympathiser, had his house set on fire.

Fr Dick McCarthy of Co. Limerick hid Treacy and Breen when there was a price on their heads. Fr Ferris, a Kerryman now eighty-six years old, was an ardent Sinn Feiner all his life. William Cosgrave, later President of the Free State, found sanctuary with the Oblate Fathers in their house at Glencree in the Wicklow Hills. He dressed as one of them and was never betrayed. Kevin O'Higgins, his assistant, also found shelter with another Order.

The hierarchy did openly condemn the efforts of the British to introduce conscription here and perhaps helped to defeat it. Many other clergy rendered good service, the details of which are now lost in the unrecorded history of those terrible days.

As a whole, the Catholic clergy welcomed the settlement with England and were staunch supporters of the Irish Free State.

12

THE PROSCRIBED Dail or Sinn Fein Parliament, most of whose members were 'on the run', was to hold a clandestine meeting in Dublin, which of course the British would be only too glad to surprise. This was in May, 1921. They had consistently warred against it since its inception. Collins asked me to keep a sharp look-out against Castle agents in the vicinity of the meeting, which was held in an old store owned by Alderman Cole. The session lasted two or three days. So I took leave for that period and spent each day patrolling in the vicinity, but saw no suspicious touts about. Truly, truth is stranger than fiction! Here was I, a member of the Castle political police, keeping watch over the rebel parliament at the behest of Michael Collins, the most hunted man in Ireland. The members duly dispersed. No inkling reached the Castle. This Dail which I protected, contained men who afterwards persecuted me and made my life a misery. Such are the turns of fortune's wheel.

A friend of Collins gave a party in a nice house in the suburbs. He invited McNamara and myself. It was a merry evening. Collins recited a ballad: 'Kelly and Burke and Shea', about Irish emigrants, which he did very well. Piaras Beasley recited another. It was of course on a patriotic theme; I remember only the refrain, 'To expiate their Saxon sins would need another Christ!' He was a slightly-built little fellow. When I looked at his lean face and smouldering dark eyes as he solemnly declaimed this hymn of hate, I couldn't help thinking; this is the fanaticism of a real revolutionary. Later I got to know him well. He was a mild and charming fellow who idolised Collins. Indeed, that could be said for most of those around Collins as he had great personal magnetism and generosity. If anyone were ill, depressed or lonely, one person never forgot; Michael Collins.

At Christmas time he had Joe O'Reilly run off his feet buying presents for everybody. He gave me a silver cigarette case wrapped in tissue paper. Others got tobacco, cuff-links or some other little gift. In the middle of his myriad tasks, he did not forget these little touches which endeared him to all. Collins left the party early that night, and Tobin and McNamara left with me in a car. When McNamara and I returned to the castle we found that all the bridges ringing Dublin had been covered by searching British patrols that night, with the sole exception of that over which we had passed.

Years later I asked Liam Tobin who was our hostess that night—a charming elderly woman—and he replied that she was in the entourage of a prominent Britisher—even now it's better to leave it at that.

Collins had astonishing contacts, but one thing is certain; the mysterious Lieutenant referred to in this connection in a life of Collins did not exist. I have Liam Tobin's word for it. Beasley was at that time the Editor (and, except for J. J. O'Connell, an able officer and Dick Mulcahy, another), probably the sole contributor of an I.R.A. underground publication known as An tOglac. This was of course a prohibited paper. Possession of it was enough to earn a man death at the hands of British forces. It contained articles on such lethal topics as ambushing, care of arms, and street fighting, as well as accounts of warlike activities. Beasley was a good journalist, so it was quite a readable little paper. The printing works that turned it out, McMahon's, was raided dozens of times by the British. Many were the makeshifts to which Beasley was driven. Publication never ceased, to the chagrin of the Castle.

My sister Eileen (who was injured in the accident which killed my brother) now joined the staff of Stack's Home Affairs office under another name. This was, of course, a hidden department. Though only a stone's throw from the castle, it was never discovered by the British. She worked there until the end with Madge Clifford, a dark-eyed beauty from Kerry. Miss Clifford (now Mrs Comer) who was Stack's secretary tells me in a letter that they had a secret office at first at 45 Henry St, Dublin: 'We lasted there a long time until one day two of the staff went out to lunch leaving me alone in the place. . . . I heard a knock at the door but it was usual for persons seeking the wireless school (on the floor above us) to enquire its location. I did not answer. In came two Auxies. "What are you doing?" one asked. I said "We are solicitors; can't you see the name on the door: 'Murray & Quirke'?" Two others came in and asked the same question; then they went upstairs. In came yet another pair and made for the inner office where we kept the files (of the Ministry of Home Affairs). I said: "Your men have already searched there." One fellow who seemed to be in charge apologised and said he hoped they did not frighten me. He was a decent sort. I asked if I could go to lunch and he replied "Of course you can", blew his whistle and they cleared off. We had one very important file and covering address book which I took but where could I put it? The street was cordoned off by the enemy at each end. I chanced an old woman dealer at a street-stall and asked would she keep it, which she did, handing it up safely later in the week. Collins' office was further down in Mary Street. We (Home Affairs) left there to go to Wellington Quay. The Republican police took over the old office and were captured there—papers and all.'

Tom Cullen, Collins' intelligence officer, who fooled Jameson about the revolvers, used to come along to our meetings with Tobin. He was a handsome man with fresh complexion and sparkling eyes. A poor shop assistant, he was a great athlete and runner. Naturally gay and intelligent, he was brave as a lion. A very likeable fellow in every way, he was a native of Wicklow. One day a prominent Sinn Feiner named R. C. Barton, also from Wicklow, was, while a prisoner—having been sentenced by court martial—being moved from the castle to Mountjoy Prison (that miscalled dungeon). It was proposed to rescue him *en route*. It was known that he would be in a covered lorry. Cullen waited at the castle gate. When this vehicle emerged, he ran as fast as his legs could carry him to Berkeley Road, a distance of two or three miles, getting there in time to alert the rescuers. They immediately held up the lorry, only to find that it contained a lot of poor devils of Tommies on their way to the glasshouse. They allowed them to continue on their dolorous journey. Barton was removed in an armoured car. Him, too, I was to meet long afterwards when he acted the part of a friend at a time when they were scarce. He was related to Erskine Childers.

Tobin and Cullen were both badly wanted men by the British. They had both met Jameson and Mulloy who, of course, reported on them. The British secret service made many efforts to trap them, though all failed. One of their closest escapes was in Vaughan's Hotel which was then a favourite roosting place for such as they. The British undoubtedly watched that place (in fact a resident spy lodged there according to Beasley). One night they sent a military raiding party to arrest them. Both men slept in a room on the top floor, and were awakened about 3 a.m. by a knocking at their door. They opened it to be confronted by a British captain and his men, who invited them to dress and come on. They spun some yarn covering up, and partly convinced the officer that this was a case of mistaken identity. Innocently enough, he told them to stay there until he went downstairs to phone. Getting speech with his superiors he was sharply told not to be a damned fool, but to go back and arrest them. On his return, the birds had flown. Admittedly they had not flown far. They were crouched on the window-sill outside, high above the street. The Captain never thought of raising the blind. They avoided Vaughan's after that.

Cullen was fond of horse-racing and often saw British secret-service men at the meetings. He used to call them tick-tack men—those nimble signallers of the track. The secret service was extremely busy at this time. The British sent some of their crack operators here. I must say they were brave men who carried their lives in their hands. As is well known (to me at any rate), a spy leads a lonely and dangerous existence full of perils, in the midst of enemies, never acknowledged by his masters, at the end thrown on the scrap-heap, if he is lucky enough to see the end. They shadowed suspects continually and kept meeting-places under surveillance, carrying out all the functions of a secret police. Working in close co-operation with the military and Auxiliaries, they had some victories. Some had seen service in other parts of the Empire. I saw a report from one dated on a Saturday which was the vigil of a Catholic feast. He said: 'A big operation must be imminent, (the natives are restless), the R.C. churches were crowded all day.'

One of the places under observation by them was a little draper's shop in Talbot Street called the Republican Outfitters. It was watched one day by a British agent called Price. He saw a prominent Volunteer officer called Sean Treacy enter. Treacy had shot his way out of Professor Carolan's house in Drumcondra some nights earlier. He and another Tipperary leader named Dan Breen had in the course of the affair killed two British military officers, one a Major Smyth. As Treacy was well known to the local R.I.C., it must be assumed that they furnished the British with his description and perhaps his photograph. Anyway, he looked a typical Volunteer and I suppose Price realised this. When Treacy emerged from the shop, Price drew a revolver and told him to put up his hands. Treacy, a very hardy and courageous man, grappled with him and took the gun away from him. Price worked in co-operation with a lorry load of Tommies who waited nearby. Seeing the two men struggling, the Tommies opened fire and killed both of them. That day in the castle, I saw various brass-hats including Colonel Winter of Intelligence standing around a big military lorry which contained a tarpaulin. Going over to them, I asked Winter, who was friendly enough, what was in the lorry. 'Sean Treacy and one of my fellows,' he replied. Many versions of this affair have been given, but the only one likely to know the truth has remained silent. McKee and several other leaders of the I.R.A. were in that shop at the time. They were decidedly unwary in their movements at that period.

After Winter retired he wrote his memoirs entitled *Winter's Tale*. He gave a good account of his service in India where he engaged in buying and selling ponies, of which he seems to have been a shrewd judge. He was a dapper little fellow with a monocle. One day as he drove to Baldonnel Military Airport, two I.R.A. men named McGuinness (not related) blazed at him and nearly put paid to his account. He was injured in one thumb and received £1,000 in the Recorder's Court. Those two Volunteers were tough men and regularly blazed at any target passing through their area in Inchicore.

Collins was furious over Treacy's death and the death of the man in charge of the military party was decreed. He was wounded that day in the Treacy episode and put in a claim for compensation. The day the claim came up, the squad attended the court to shoot him. An armoured car backed slowly into the courtyard and he emerged. The place swarmed with armed soldiers. I waved the squad away. He received a substantial sum and faded out shortly afterwards. Treacy and Breen were original members of the squad and were really tough men. The British had a reward of £1,000 on Breen's head after the Soloheadbeg affair. It was unclaimed.

The Auxies dealt the Dublin Brigade a severe blow in Pearse Street where six Volunteers were shot. One, a poor devil of a cobbler named Traynor was captured, tried by court martial and sentenced to death. Breen had captured a District Inspector Potter in Tipperary and offered to exchange him for Traynor but the British refused. Traynor was hanged in April, 1921. Potter was told he would be shot next morning at dawn. He wrote a poignant letter to his wife and was shot. It was one of the most terrible tragedies of that terrible time. This letter and the dead man's watch were found in Collins' secret office in Mary Street, Dublin, which the Auxies raided. Collins was about to return them to Potter's widow. After the war Potter's relative visited Breen, when the latter told him that no one regretted his father's death more than he did.

F Company of the Auxies of the castle made themselves very busy. They visited a poor locksmith named Carroll who had two sons on the run. They warned him that if they did not surrender he would be shot. Later they shot him and put a label on his body: 'Spies beware I.R.A.'

Next day I received a note from Collins: 'Concentrate on MAYEM.' This man was said to be the killer of Carroll. He used to go to lunch daily at 1 p.m. I knew him well. I sent word to Collins to send a man to meet me; I would attend and identify our quarry. Having observed that he kept regular hours, I took up position outside his quarters next day at lunch-time. Across the road, Joe Guilfoyle, a member of the squad, sat astride his bicycle. As this was merely a matter of identification, he carried no firearms, which was just as well as events turned out. To my surprise lunch-time came and went and there was no sign of our man. As hanging about there was highly dangerous for a man like Guilfoyle, I went across the road and told him to clear off; to return tomorrow at the same hour. He told me that another member of the squad, Paddy Caldwell, was watching for our man at his lunch place and that he would go there and tell him to withdraw. He cycled away. Mayem's anxious relative saw Caldwell in the street and immediately concluded that it boded ill for him. As the watcher was joined by a man with a bicycle, the relative hesitated no longer, but immediately phoned to Mayem.

As both men chatted, an armoured car came flying up the street, Mayem sticking his head out and waving his revolver invited the two squad men inside. Back to the Auxies' H.Q. in Beggars Bush they went, Mayem locking them in a cell while he went to lunch, in the mess this time. While he was absent, Caldwell ate a note-book which contained such deadly data as the numbers of Hamar Greenwood's, McCready's and Tudor's cars with that of Mayem. He also chewed up the leather covers. That was the only lunch he got that day. Mayem returned in good form after lunch and started interrogating them separately.

Guilfoyle gave a fake name and address—these were owned by a neutral citizen (probably pro-British) who was not aware of this interesting exchange of identities. Of course he put up some other yarn to account for his meeting with Caldwell. The details of this I've forgotten. Anyway, he found himself in the armoured car again with Mayem on their way to check his name and address. In answer to his knock the real owner of the name came to the door. Mayem, who wore military uniform, enquired whether Joe was living there. The man was just about to deny it when he caught sight of Guilfoyle's agonised face. He told Mayem that such was the case, though he had never before seen or heard of Guilfoyle. Guilfoyle was released but Caldwell spent the next three months in prison. Caldwell I've never met, though he phoned me the other day giving details of the episode which I'd forgotten.

I think that man, whose name I've forgotten, was a real hero. Waiters, hotel porters and other humble folk knew Collins, Tobin,

Cullen and other leaders. They never breathed a word whereas they could have commanded a fortune by betraying them. No monument exists to such people. They are never mentioned. History ignores them. They got no pensions, no medals, and no thanks. To my mind they are most deserving of praise, who by their loyalty and devotion defeated every effort of the enemy. The sort of guerilla struggle which went on in Ireland depends, of course, on the active support of the populace. Where this is not forthcoming, defeat for the weaker side is inevitable.

The British propagandists, including the lords and dukes, pretended that this was a campaign of murder; that the rebels should 'come out and fight'. It is a very foolish fighter who obeys the advice of his enemy! Nineteen hundred and sixteen provided an example of coming out, and taught people like Collins that a handful had no chance openly battling with an empire. It was a different story, of course, during the Second World War. Then the lords lauded the resistance to Hitler's hoardes and found no difficulty in putting them on the side of the angels. All their battles were fought on paper.

The war raged with ferocity in Cork City (which the Auxies burned down) and county. Collins, when we met him, used to be thrilled when he learnt of feats against the British there. Three vigorous leaders he admired were Liam Lynch, a lion-hearted man who was O.C. of 1st Southern Division, Tom Barry, a column leader of genius, and Sean Hales, another. Barry gave the Auxiliaries a terrible beating in one ambush, killing about fourteen. And this only a couple of miles from their stronghold. What struck me at the time was the rapid transit of news to Collins. Happenings in remote areas of West Cork were reported to him in a matter of half-an-hour.

I have mentioned the Dail Loan and the British efforts to smash it. At this time they had many bones to pick with Liam Lynch, their most dangerous enemy in the South. He was a native of East Limerick, a poor shop assistant. A namesake (no relation) from the same area who belonged to the political wing of Sinn Fein came to Dublin with Dail Loan moneys he had collected locally and handed them over to Collins. He stayed at a small hotel practically across the road from the castle—it is called

104

Exchange Hotel. The British intelligence people got the idea that this man was Liam Lynch who was a thorn in their side. A party of them raided the place in the middle of the night and shot the man dead. Collins was furious. Next day I received a note from him asking me urgently to make enquiries as to the killers.

13

IN EVERY police station is kept a large ledger called the Occurrence Book. In this is entered every happening which comes to the notice of the station sergeant on duty. These men who do an eight-hour shift are all intelligent fellows who have passed a fairly stiff examination and are senior N.C.O.s. It is said that the R.I.C. Occurrence Book had a note of the state of the weather daily like a ship's log. This is not as crazy as it sounds because the weather could have a bearing on crime. Abe Lincoln, when at the bar, got his client off once by proving that on a certain night there was no moon.

As the Exchange Hotel was in B Division, I called at once to College Street Station where I had previously served. The station sergeant on duty was a friend of mine and he asked me to relieve him while he went to the canteen for a drink. Opening the Occurrence Book, I read that 'at such and such an hour, on such a date, Captain Usilade, Army Staff, Dublin Castle, 'phoned to state that he and others had raided the Exchange Hotel at 2 a.m. to arrest a suspect named Lynch. He had opened fire on them with a revolver, and they had returned the fire, killing him.'

In due course, I conveyed a copy of this entry to Collins. His staff was, like myself and McNamara, patiently compiling a list of British secret-service men, especially those who had figured in episodes like that above. A terrible retribution awaited them.

The British, having prohibited inquests in order to cover up these crimes, there was none on poor Lynch. The British had a tight censorship on newspapers. Lynch was an elderly man who, though a sympathiser, was never in the army wing of Sinn Fein. It was a brazen lie that he had a gun or fired shots.

Talking of Occurrence Books brings me back again to the G-man's diary. This was a large calf-bound volume which was kept in the castle office. Here was entered an account of how the day had been spent, with mention of all suspects seen, where they went and the company they kept. Most of the suspects mentioned by the G-men were 'old cods' who had long lost any revolutionary ardour they'd had, if they ever had it. All the same there was always a danger a G-man might stumble on something, as they knew a lot of people. So I made it my business to read these journals regularly. They were generally filled at 6 p.m. each day.

One night about 9 p.m. I was busily going through them when the door opened silently. Chief Inspector Bruton entered. I had not heard his approach as he wore rubber-soled shoes. He looked at me in a peculiar manner: 'You're working late, Dave.' Feeling the tension in the air, I muttered some excuse about being delayed. He went away. If he had come nearer he would have seen that I had open before me the diary of a detective sergeant which was no affair of mine.

Bruton, afraid to go outside the castle, used to come to the office at night out of sheer boredom and to kill time. The only time he left the place was on Sundays when he went to Mass, accompanied by an escort and by two other officials also on the danger list. It was decided to shoot the three of them, so the squad attended outside the church one Sunday. As I had been 'press-ganged' to go with them that day, the affair was called off. Next Sunday the squad turned up there to learn that they were at another church. A week after that they went there and found that the officials were at yet another church. It got so farcical in the end that the newsboys, those sharp-eyed gamins, used to shout: 'Misters! They're not here today!' In the event, they escaped unscathed.

I have related how Collins stored Broy's documents from the G Division in Brunswick Street. These were kept in sacks at the flat of Miss Eileen McGrane, an ardent Sinn Fein sympathiser who lived in Dawson Street. They were discovered by a British raiding party there on 3rd December 1920 and brought to the castle. It became clear to the British that Broy was the culprit, he being the typist at the time in question. Soon an armoured car called to the detective office in Brunswick Street. Broy was at tea. Two Tommy officers came in, arrested him and conveyed him to Arbour Hill. This was a military dungeon equivalent to the Tower of London. It contained many cells, including a glasshouse for Tommies. It was freely rumoured that Broy was to be executed. In the temper of the enemy at the time, it was a distinct possibility. McNamara and I met Collins in Gay's house. He was perturbed over Broy. He told us he would organise his rescue; the odds meant nothing to him; he revelled in forlorn hopes. And this was one.

Knowing what his reaction to Broy's arrest would be, I had been poking about Arbour Hill, sizing up the possibilities. Now I asked Collins did he know anything of the defences there. He admitted he did not. 'Well,' I said, 'there are at least four Lewis [machine] guns manned by "old sweats" [long-service soldiers], an alert, picked garrison. The surrounding walls are ten feet high topped by barbed wire; there is an alarm signal which can be heard miles away. Within a stone's throw are two large military barracks with hundreds of troops and a battery of eighteen-pounders. Anyone who shows his nose near that place will be chatting with his forefathers in seconds.' Collins was horrified. 'What'll we do so?' he asked us.

Since the arrest, McNamara and I had given the matter a lot of thought. We told Collins of our solution. No bones would be broken if it worked and it would cost nothing to try it. We thought the framing of the case against Broy would be handled by Detective Chief Inspector Joe Supple. We added that he could be frightened, so that he would fail to drive home the charge. McNamara told us the Chief Inspector used to start the day well by attending Mass in Mount Argus near where he lived. We told Collins to have it conveyed to him that if he went on with the case, the best thing he could do was to pick out a nice shady spot for himself in Mount Jerome Cemetery across the way, for that is where he would be. Collins was delighted. 'By God,' he said, 'I'll go up there tonight!' This meant a ride on the old bicycle of at least ten miles and he cleared off at once.

Though Broy was in military custody we thought that they would foist his case upon the G-men. Supple was the most likely recipient of this unwanted task, he being a sort of executive officer in Broy's office. We didn't ask Supple, though!

Collins' mission that night was to interview a man who would convey the message to Supple. As the latter was leaving the church next morning, a polished gentleman who happened to be passing, beckoned to him. Joe, a sparely-built, goat-faced little man, came flying over, doffing his bowler. In the office he wore glasses of powerful magnification. When he spoke to one he lowered his head to clear the view. As old Sergeant Gibney, a witty fellow, said: 'You'd think he was going to puck [i.e. butt] you.' That morning he was flanked by his wife and daughter. Once I heard him in the office ask another G-man what was Collins' rank in the 'Sinn Feiners'. When the man replied, 'Minister of Finance', Joe's comment was, 'Minister for Murder'. He had been walking the tight-rope politically for a long time, sending out others to get shot, but now—thank Heaven—those political police had been removed to the castle, leaving him in peace.

He did not realise that now the precipice was opening at his feet. He asked the urbane beckoner what he could do for him. 'You can do nothing for me, Mr Supple,' he replied. 'But I have a grave warning to give you! It concerns someone called Broy, of whom I know nothing. I am to tell you that if you go on with the case against him, you will be shot!' If Joe had not been grabbed by his poor wife and daughter, he would have fallen on the spot. Muttering to the man who had transmitted this sombre signal, he was frog-marched home by those devoted ladies.

A thousand curses on the Castle and on the political police! Just when he had washed his hands of those wretches they had returned to plague him. And to put him in peril of his life! And he knew that this was no idle threat. In fact he was lucky to get any warning. Smyth, Hoey, Barton hadn't got any; just volleys fired at them. Now, Supple was no fool; fools don't get to be chief detective inspectors. The only man in the G Division he was afraid of was Detective Inspector McCabe, a Protestant Loyalist. Though by no means a brilliant detective, McCabe would instantly spot any fancy foot-work that Joe would perform in Broy's case. Perhaps have him fired like McFeely was. 'Yes, the first step was to disarm McCabe. But how?' Something had to be done and quickly. The British were pressing him to get on with the case. Supple came into the detective office in Brunswick Street that morning. He was very pale; had aged a good deal recently. His hands shook. When McCabe, a stoutly built blusterer, came in, the Inspector on duty told him to report to the Chief Inspector. When he did so, Joe locked the door after he had entered. He told McCabe that he had been warned that *both* of them would be shot if Broy was convicted, but would not say from what source he had gleaned this dread news. He convinced McCabe of its truth. Action followed at once. Waiting until the others had gone off about their business, McCabe and Supple armed themselves with two large pokers, broke open Broy's old trunk or box, also his locker which contained nothing but groceries, and burned everything they found, including a P.O. savings bank book. It took Broy ages before he could get the P.O. to recoup him his few pounds. To this day I do not know what excuse the two made to the British. It must have been water-tight, for Broy was never brought to trial and both lived to draw their pensions. Of course McCabe being what he was, would not have incurred Collins' wrath. Actually McCabe lived quite near me in his old age. He used to glare at me as he was wheeled by in a bath-chair. I often intended to ask him how they evaded the issue, but as he grew somewhat irascible of later years, I refrained.

After some time Broy was released on bail and the matter ended there. Mac and myself thought it was a great improvement on rows of dead men at Arbour Hill.

If this scheme had failed we had another string to our bow. Broy's predecessor as typist was Pat McCarthy, a clever, able Corkman. Sent to London once for a course of detective instruction which was attended by detectives from all the colonies and dependencies, then the Empire, he passed the final examination, getting first place. He was an enormously stout, suave fellow with a terrific head of hair like a wig. When first the G-men were being attacked, Pat, being a shrewd fellow, decided to hedge his bet, like Mizner who, dying, told them to send for a priest, a parson and a rabbi.

He had a teacher brother in Dublin who was a mild, parlour

Sinn Feiner. He sent the brother to Collins to tell him that he, Pat, had nothing to do with political police but was merely indexing cabs. (The carriage office which does that sort of thing is next door to the detective office.) Collins heard what the man had to say. Then he produced a little docket from a card-index system. This contained the name, address, usual haunts and habits of a prominent Sinn Feiner, all set out in his brother's beautiful script. He handed it to the man. 'Ask him what has that got to do with taxicabs?' The poor fellow left in a hurry and went straight to the detective office where he told the Detective Sergeant, his brother Pat.

I was there that day, knowing nothing of these events. Pat, ashen-faced, shaking like a leaf, asked me to escort him to the castle. He was going to resign. He feared being attacked on the way. I was sorry for the poor devil and asked him did he not feel well. The irony of this remark struck me afterwards when I heard what had happened. We walked to the castle. I've never seen a man in a more terrible panic.

He cleared out at once and went to London. If the Chief Inspector had not been scared away, Broy's defence was going to be that ex-Sergeant Pat McCarthy was the villain of the piece. In pursuance of this finesse, Collins had sent a man to McCarthy's lodgings in London with a single ticket for the U.S.A. and a warning to leave at once, which he did. Amusingly enough, though not for Pat, he was met at the other side by Liam Pedlar to whom he had earlier given six months for making a seditious speech of which he, McCarthy, had taken a shorthand note. However, they found him a job in the U.S.A. and he sat out the war there. When the British sought him in London as a witness against Broy, the fact that he had scooted began to look to them as if there were something in Broy's contention.

After the show was over, we took him back and made amends for bumping him about so much, by promoting him to Super-intendent. Many years later, at home in the castle, I was enter-taining two old hands telling them of McCarthy's tribulations, whereat they laughed heartily. Incredibly enough, the door opened and McCarthy entered. He lived to draw his pension and is now dead.

Another G-man, a sergeant, a married man, had, it is said, picked out men for British firing squads after the 1916 rebellion. This may not have been true, but it is a fact that Collins had ordered his execution. The squad only awaited a favourable opportunity to kill him. Often I was sent with him on duty. We shall call him Duncan. One day we were at Kingsbridge terminus and I saw Kennedy of Tralee talking to another man. When he saw me he came over for a chat. Duncan stood aside. After Kennedy had left, he asked me, 'Who is your friend, Dave?' 'He is Kennedy of the Kerry County Council,' I said, adding cautiously that he took no part in politics. This was, of course true of the Jekyll but not of the Hyde. 'His pal does, then,' he said. 'He is Dinny Callaghan, an I.R.B. man.' As I had ignored Callaghan, who was not known to me, I truthfully told Duncan that I'd never seen him before. Duncan said no more about it, but I imagine that if he had told Bruton of the incident, it might start a hare; give Bruton suspicions that I couldn't afford just then.

Regularly, of a morning, I used to call at his house for Duncan. His devoted wife worried continually about the danger he was in. 'My God, Mr Neligan, aren't they terrible times?' And she used to add, lowering her voice, 'What'll become of us, if anything happens to him?' Knowing that he was nearly as good as dead already, I made up my mind to try and save his life. The snag was that I could see no way out of this terrible dilemma, simply bristling with horns. If I told Duncan he was going to be shot, he and Bruton would naturally want to know where I'd got my information and what was the answer to that? If I'd told Collins: 'For God's sake leave him alone,' he would upbraid me for saving a man who had gone out of his way to war on the I.R.A. And it was true. As things stood, Collins was justified in striking the man down, if bloodshed is ever justified.

Lying awake at night in the castle, I turned the thing over in my mind without getting anywhere near a solution. Time was running out fast. One morning, after I'd had a sleepless night, Bruton told me to call for Duncan. We were to go on duty together. After the usual salutation from his wife we started off. I said to him, 'Where are we going?' 'Making enquiries,' he said.

This meant that he was chasing political suspects with a view to having them arrested. I turned on him furiously. The wakeful hours had my temper on edge. 'These enquiries will soon lead to your death!' I shouted at him. He was astounded and turned very pale. 'Why do you say that, Dave?' 'I was in a pub last night and I heard two fellows saying that you will be shot. Why don't you tell Bruton that it's too dangerous for you to go out making enquiries? He doesn't go out himself.'

His lips trembled. 'Will you come with me, Dave, and tell Bruton?' 'Yes,' I said. It was true enough, what I'd said, with this difference, that I knew the two men and was in their company in Bannon's pub. We went to Bruton who heard what I had to say, believed it, and agreed that Duncan should stay inside, where he gave no trouble to anyone and lasted out to the end. I told the squad that he was too frightened to come out. Being of long service, he knew a great number of people in the city and there was always a danger that someone would tip him off about I.R.A. activities, but confined to the castle, he could do no harm. He had plenty of company there. Hordes of officials holed up there and spent their evenings walking about, some wearing steel waistcoats. I never knew who most of them were, but they clearly feared going outside.

One evening a senior police officer directed me to wait at the main gate of Dublin Castle to usher in the Postmaster of a suburban city P.O. 'who had important information about the Sinn Feiners'. Collins, on being informed, directed Joe Leonard and C. Dalton, two squad men, to shoot the man at the gate. Fortunately, he did not turn up and no action was taken against him afterwards.

Later, I often wondered: (a) how those two were going to get away at midnight when the city was alive with patrols and armoured cars enforcing* 10 p.m. curfew, and (b) what explanation was I going to make as to the sudden demise of the informant. This was one of the hair-raising episodes of the time!

* Curfew commenced in Dublin on 23rd February 1920.

14

ONE OF our new entrants in the G Division, Fenton, was a man who had been in every station in the service. The reason was that the poor fellow had not much sense and could not get on with people. In addition, he was quarrelsome and possessed a violent temper. A very credulous man, he believed every ridiculous yarn he was told. Once, under transfer to another station, his comrades told him that the bed in his new station was damp. 'What should I do?' he asked. They told him to go to the Gresham Hotel for the night, send the bill to the Superintendent, which he did. The Superintendent was not amused. The man was fined £2 and had to pay the hotel too.

Another morning he had just retired from a tour of night duty and was asleep. His mates told a boy messenger he was due for duty, so the lad called him. The enraged P.C. flung the lad through a window and was dismissed. If the poor fellow had been left alone he would have done all right, but unfortunately men in barracks delight in cruelly ill-treating the like of him. It is a stupid and silly attitude which I've often seen. Children of a larger growth, indeed.

Tommy O'Shaughnessy lived in Fitzwilliam Square. Often I escorted him to and from Green Street Courthouse where he sat. 'Larry' O'Neill, the Lord Mayor of Dublin, often sat on the Bench with Tommy. I regarded this as a piece of window-dressing on Tommy's part. The Lord Mayor had no function except the old-fashioned ill-defined courtesy title of the 'city's chief magistrate'. O'Neill was well known to be a Sinn Fein sympathiser (General McCready jeered about him a lot in his book). The Recorder's public remarks about conditions were always extremely guarded and inoffensive. Generally he confined himself to saying that he deplored the unsettled state of affairs, especially as it meant a burden on the unfortunate ratepayers, and ended with a pious hope that things would soon improve. These honeyed words were echoed by the Lord Mayor. Tommy hardly ever spoke to me except once or twice when he asked my opinion about cases he'd heard and politely listened to my reply.

Once, however, as we passed Higgins' pub around the corner from his home, he stood in the street until I came up. 'When are you fellows going to catch the scoundrel Collins?' If I had answered truthfully it would be to say, 'Open the door of Higgins' pub there and catch him yourself,' for I knew that Collins was in there waiting for me. However, I muttered that it was only a question of time until we laid him by the heels. 'I sincerely hope so,' said the Recorder; 'we met today [i.e. the Privy Council] and made an Order in Council giving you fellows power to search suspicious persons in the street.' That was the last I heard of such an order.

The Recorder was an admirer and collector of silver snuff-boxes of which he had a beautiful and valuable collection. Every evening on his way home from the courts, he spent hours rummaging in the old curiosity shops along the quays, often picking up an addition to his collection. No money changed hands though. The shopkeepers were only too glad to present his Lordship with such objects, for reasons best known to themselves.

Tommy's son was a barrister. He was a harmless poor fellow who got an occasional brief to appear before his father, until the Bar Council put a stop to it. Once in a civil action he appeared. Tim Healy was on the other side. Healy made a point which he thought might gain him the verdict, but as Tommy saw the son's case going down the drain, he said to Healy, 'I can't see your point, Mr Healy.' 'No,' muttered Tim to his beard, 'the sun is in your eyes.' Collins wanted to shoot the son but I dissuaded him. He had been foolish.

In court, another day when I was there, Healy was defending a woman publican from the hills who was 'up' for selling drink after hours. A young R.I.C. sergeant gave his evidence, from which it was clear that an offence had been committed. The publican had already been convicted by a magistrate, and this was her appeal. Healy rose to cross-examine. So far as the offence was concerned he had not a leg to stand on. His *forte* was not so much knowledge of the law, but an abusive and persuasive tongue. He pitched into the Sergeant at once. 'Didn't you arrive at this poor widow's door at 1 a.m.? Terrorising her and her helpless orphans! Shouting at the top of your voice: "I'm the Sergeant of Rathfarnham!" You'd think you were the Autocrat of All the Russias', and a lot more to the same effect. I could see beads of perspiration on the brow of the poor witness. Healy followed up this barrage with volleys of questions, some idiotic, but all designed to confuse and discomfit the witness. These fallacious arguments, irrelevancy and flights of fancy which are part of a barrister's stock-in-trade are known to them as making bricks without straw. The conviction was reversed.

To the Law Library attached to the Four Courts occasionally came an old barrister who'd never had a brief but was wildly hoping that the British would raise him to the bench. He only turned up when a vacancy appeared likely. One morning Healy arrived there and asked the Librarian, 'Which of the Judges is dying?' 'What in hell do you mean?' replied the official, 'none is dying.' Tim indicated the old fellow in a corner. 'Don't you see the banshee?'

At this time I had an illustrious namesake in Cork: Sir David Neligan was Recorder there. He had a weakness for Latin tags. Once he heard an action between two old farmers who had a dispute over a boundary on their mountain holding (a very frequent bone of contention, sometimes leading to mortal combat). When the learned Recorder had given his verdict, he turned to Mr Harte Barry, solicitor, a witty Corkman who survived into his nineties. 'Mr Harte Barry, has your Client never heard of the adage: De minimis non curat lex?' (The law ignores trifles.) 'Yes, my Lord, they hear it every day. It's the one topic on top of Knocknamuck mountain!' The last time I heard that story, it had emigrated to the Cotswolds!

Following on some weak-kneed decision by the Judges involving the execution of a Volunteer, the Volunteer executive ordered the kidnapping of all the Judges in Dublin including the

116

Recorder. Collins asked me to compile their addresses, which I did. However, the job was called off, for which I was grateful. O'Shaughnessy was an old man and probably would not have survived rough usage.

O'Shaughnessy had a rival at the bar before he was elevated to the bench. This man had a brother who was a peer. A vacancy occurred. The Peer's brother won in a canter. Meeting O'Shaughnessy later he said: 'O'Shaughnessy, I had a man of your name before me the other day for rape. I was wondering was he a brother of yours?' 'I've no brother,' said Tommy; 'if I'd a brother I'd have been on the bench long ago.'

Tim Healy was a native of Bantry in West Cork. He started life as a railway clerk at 10s. per week. Becoming adept at shorthand he got a job as private secretary to Parnell, whom he afterwards left in the lurch. Then he became a barrister and an M.P. of the Irish Parliamentary Party. Several of his fellow townsmen started life in the same bracket as he and became wealthy. A man asked him: 'How is it that all of you Bantry gang started with nothing and struck it rich?' Tim scratched his white beard. 'Ah, well!' says he, 'you know the way it is down there; when a fellow gets to be fourteen he gets a map of the world and a kick in the pants!'

It is said that the art of cross-examination consists in knowing when to stop. A barrister was cross-examining an old farmer in the provinces. The lawyer's father, who came from the same quarter, had a dubious reputation. The barrister asked the witness: 'Aren't you the biggest blackguard in the countryside?' No reply was forthcoming. 'Do you know any bigger ruffian than yourself?' 'No,' says the man, 'unless your own old dad!' Laughter in court.

The British packed the Irish Bench with ex-Crown prosecutors and political henchmen. How true is the French saying: The more things change, the more they remain the same.

The Recorder's daughter was about to marry a British major. It was the last marriage to be celebrated in the Chapel Royal, Dublin Castle (then a Protestant church). Tommy gave me the list of guests invited. It included Sir Hamar Greenwood, Chief Secretary for Ireland; Sir John Anderson and Mr Cope, Under-Secretaries; Generals McCready, Tudor and all the high-ups at the castle. I gave the list to Collins, who glanced at it and said to me: 'We'll plug the bloody lot of them!' I said it was a fine idea.

Tommy, the bridegroom and I went to Collinstown Military Camp a few days before the wedding, as the best man was stationed there—a captain. I had tea and cold meat in the sergeant's mess. The Major was a charming fellow and we had a chat once or twice. The night before the wedding one of the celebrating guests got into a row and was arrested. When I told the station sergeant at College Street who he was he was released speedily; that officer's words to me being: 'Get him to hell out of here before I'm sacked.'

The wedding was duly celebrated and everyone trooped off to Tommy's house at Fitzwilliam Square for the reception. I looked out of the window. Pacing about in twos and threes were all the squad and the active-service unit, accompanied by Liam Tobin and Rory O'Connor. I went out to them. 'For God's sake go away!' I said. 'Those fellows haven't turned up, but sent their private secretaries.' They asked me who was in there and I said, 'Nobody but the bridegroom and a poor devil of a captain from the Duke of Wellington's Regiment—he was the best man.' They told me that no one but Collins could 'call off the job'. I asked, 'Where is he?' and they said he was in a pub just outside the building now housing Dail Eireann, the parliament house. They accompanied me there.

Collins was sitting at a table upstairs. 'How did it go, Dave?' 'It didn't go'; no one turned up except the bridgroom and best man. The bridegroom has nothing to do with the British Army here. He is a decent fellow and is employed in the Inter-Allied Commission in Germany.' 'How do you know that?' he asked. 'There is the label off his luggage.' I had pulled it off a suitcase in the hall on my way out. It bore the name of the officer and of a Cologne hotel. Collins turned to Tobin and Rory: 'Call off the job!' Back in the house, Tommy dished out champagne. I had a glass for the first time.

The Chief of Staff of the Volunteers at this time was Dick Mulcahy. The British wanted him badly but he managed always to be a jump ahead of them. On the night of 10th November 1920, he had a narrow escape at the home of Professor Hayes, an

118

ardent supporter. Mulcahy, who earlier in the night, had fallen off his old bicycle and had had his teeth smashed, heard the ominous ratatat at the door in the wee hours. He shot out through a skylight and ran along the roofs in imminent danger of breaking his neck. A few doors away he dived through another skylight, frightening the wits out of a poor Jew and his wife who had been peacefully sleeping. They begged for mercy but Mulcahy soon pacified them. Back in Hayes's a British Army captain was examining Dick's paper. They were plans of Birmingham Gas Works and Liverpool Docks, which the I.R.A. planned to blow up. More interesting still was a cheque for a few hundred pounds which somebody cashed early next morning with the help of his pistol. He sent the Sergeant-Major for reinforcements. Seeing the old bike outside the man mounted it but was soon flung off. He wandered away and the reinforcements never arrived. A British staff officer paid tribute to the professional competence displayed by Mulcahy who knew Sandhurst only as a dot on the map. Needless to say Mulcahy did not get his money back! Hayes spent the next nine months in jail and was lucky to escape so lightly.

I once mentioned to him that Collins told me a certain I.R.A. officer of high rank had resigned as he had a conscientious objection to shooting the Tans. 'Ah no, Dave,' said Dick in his quiet voice, 'he didn't resign but he built a dug-out on top of the highest mountain in the Province and neither the enemy nor ourselves could find him until the Truce.'

Another good man was Sean McMahon, Quartermaster-General of the Volunteers. This was a highflown title for a job with more kicks than ha'pence. A quartermaster-general is the housekeeper of an army; supplying them with everything they need, with emphasis, of course, on warlike stores. In conventional armies he can call on armament factories, arsenals, wholesalers for his needs. None of these were available to McMahon: he had to conjure them out of the air! The British took good care that such material did not reach the I.R.A. Once, McMahon placed an order for a consignment of Tommy guns in the U.S.A. factory. The British had an agent there who promptly tipped them off. The cases were 'accidentally' found by a policeman at the docks and seized. It is to be presumed that the cop's palms were well greased on the occasion: guns being packed in it.

However, McMahon stuck with the job. Such was the strain on him that his hair turned white before he was thirty. A gentle, born soldier, he had not a single enemy. One of his assistants, reading that a man had been riddled with bullets, protested volubly against such waste of rounds that were scarcer than diamonds: 'Blast them!' says he: 'riddled with bullets! Where the hell do they think we're going to get them?' McMahon managed to lay hands on two machine-guns but these precious objects remained in wraps except for one skirmish. Small bomb-factories were set up in back streets in Dublin but their output was puny. The principal source of supply for small arms ammunition was poor British Tommies who sold them and risked court martial thereby.

Paddy Sheehan, an old neighbour of mine, whom I had contacted and through whom I had offered to work for the Volunteers was in and out of prison until the end. His home broken up and his wife and children suffering: that was the case, too, with his brother Jack, a staunch patriot, like his whole family, all their lives. Paddy took the pro-Treaty side after the Truce and rejoined the Civil Service from which the British had sacked him after 1916. Curiously enough, we both wound up our official careers in the same building as 'displaced persons' in the Land Commission. Standing at his graveside, I thought: this man suffered greatly and not altogether at the hands of the foreign enemy. His brother Jack, having weathered many storms is now retired and seventy-eight years old. Their house in Co. Limerick was a centre of all rebel activity and amongst the distinguished visitors (unwilling this time) was General Lucas,* a British officer captured by the I.R.A. in Cork. He was held captive for a long time but was released eventually, in July 1920. The British did not employ him again. Another Templeglantine man, Maurice Collins, fought in the Four Courts in 1916 and was 'on the run' for years. He is now eighty years old, hale and hearty.

When Lloyd George was Prime Minister there lived in London an able Irishman, a good friend of mine, who was a staff-man on a financial paper. Afterwards, under an Irish Government, he was

* He played tennis while a captive, and poached game at night.

in the Civil Service. Though a sympathiser, he was perhaps not a Volunteer, at least not on the active list at the time.

One fine day, he and a few friends decided to go for a stroll in the country outside London. Seeing a nicely wooded park they walked through it. Several men in bowler hats seized them and bundled them into cars, bringing them to Scotland Yard. Unwittingly, they had chosen the grounds of Chequers, the country house of the Premier for their walk!

Mr Basil Thompson, the head of the Special Branch, interviewed them separately. He was alone in the room. They satisfied him that nothing sinister attached to their perambulations through the wood. He told them they were free. The Irishman, a clever fellow, on his way out recollected that the answer to one of the questions was rather obscure, so he went back to elucidate the matter to Thompson. He found that a gorgeous blonde had emerged from behind a screen and was reading to Thompson a verbatim report of his answers. Lloyd George, of course, got a first-hand account of the wonderful capture.

Sir William Norwood, the Commissioner of the London Police, found himself carpeted before the Prime Minister next day. Lloyd George was in a towering rage. He glared at Norwood. 'Why was I not notified of the arrest of those Irishmen,' he demanded. The official replied that they had satisfied Thompson as to their innocence but the Prime Minister would not be mollified. It is possible that he distrusted the heads of the police just as he did F. M. Haig and General Robertson who had described him to Haig as a 'real bad 'un'.

However that may be, Thompson read of his dismissal in the evening paper. Old Sir William resigned in protest. Thus was brought about the fall of Thompson which in turn was caused by the unreasonable attitude of the Premier. The Irishman told me personally of this incident which was confirmed by my reading of Sir William Norwood's memoirs wherein the facts are clearly set out.

The shooting of Lloyd George was mooted more than once in high I.R.A. circles, but never sanctioned. One of those who favoured it also thought up a scheme for bombing the crowds leaving the London theatres, but this was turned down as preposterous.

15

FOR A long time, Collins and his staff, including McNamara and myself, had been patiently collecting details of the British secret service. Of all the Dublin uniformed police, only six were working for Collins. I shall name them here: T. Neary from Roscommon; two brothers named Culhane from Limerick; Mannix and O'Sullivan, Kerrymen; and Matt Byrne from Kildare. Those men, when on night-duty, used to stop pedestrians out after curfew. These of course often were secret agents provided with curfew passes. It never struck them, though, that a policeman on the beat might be interested otherwise than in their breach of curfew regulations. Maids, clerks and porters in hotels and boarding houses observed lodgers who seemed to lead a nocturnal existence. Mails had been examined, suspicious persons asking questions and watching premises had been noted, and men shadowing suspects had themselves been shadowed. Collins was especially interested in those who had carried out the killings like that of Carroll, the old locksmith, and Lynch in the Exchange Hotel.

On Saturday night, 20th November 1920, Tobin and Cullen asked myself and McNamara to the Gaiety Theatre. They told us that those agents were to be shot next morning. In a box nearby were two or three of them with women. Cullen asked me was I going to Croke Park, a hurling and football pitch, next day. There was an important match on. I said: 'No damn fear, and don't you go there either!' He asked 'Why not?' and I said that if those men got shot in the morning the Tans and Auxies would surely revenge themselves by shooting up Croke Park.

The following morning Chief Inspector Bruton came into our

mess-room in the castle while we breakfasted. 'Terrible work in the city this morning,' he said with white face. 'A whole lot of British officers shot.' Squads of armed Volunteers had broken down bedroom doors in various houses about the city with sledge-hammers 'borrowed' the night before from railway workshops. About fifteen or sixteen officers and agents had been shot, some of them in bed. One barricaded his door and thereby saved his life; a wife trying to save her husband was killed accidentally. One of those sought was out for a stroll and escaped.

Captain Usilade who had phoned about Lynch was amongst the dead. One of Collins' intelligence men went with one squad; he had the macabre task of searching the bodies for papers. As three or four were shot in that house, he promptly fainted and had to be carried out.

Accompanied by a colleague, I went to the Recorder's home. In the next street, two British Army ambulances waited. R.A.M.C. men emerged with stretchers on which lay inert figures. Auxies arrived in lorries and held up idlers who gaped at the street-corner. That morning, two Auxies came on the scene, running into an I.R.A. squad at about 9 a.m. in a nearby street. The squad brought them into a garden and shot them. They were very unlucky to have come visiting at that particular moment.

In the castle panic reigned. For the next week the gates were choked with incoming traffic—all the military, their wives and agents who had escaped the onslaught sought protection within the walls. A bed was not to be found for love or money. Terror gripped the invincible spy system of England. An agent in the castle whose pals had been victims shot himself. He was buried with the others, in England. The attack was so well organised, so unexpected, and so ruthlessly executed that the effect was paralysing. This was bringing it home to them, in earnest. It can be said that the enemy never recovered from the blow. While some of the worst of the killers escaped, they were thoroughly frightened. Hundreds of Tans and Auxies concentrated on Croke Park, opening fire with rifles and machine-guns on the densely-packed crowd, killing and wounding a great number. In spite of my warning, Cullen went there and had to climb a tall fence to get away. The British agents received a state funeral in London.

Late on that Saturday night, 20th November, Dick McKee, the O.C. Dublin Brigade, was arrested in Gloucester Street, Dublin, with two companions, P. Clancy, also a leader, and Clune, a sympathiser from Co. Clare. The British must have been tipped off about their location; it was no fluke that they went to that house. It was said that a local who was a redcap gave them away.

On Monday, 22nd November, I had an appointment with Thornton in a church adjacent to the castle, called SS. Michael and John's. It is a very quiet, hidden place in a back street. He turned up with six or seven others. He told me that Collins was terribly upset by the arrest of McKee and Clancy. He thought they were in the Bridewell, a prison attached to the district court at the rear of the Four Courts. He said Collins wanted me to search the Bridewell for them. If I were exposed as a result, he would see that I was sent to America. Those men with Thornton were to attempt the rescue of McKee in the event that they were in the Bridewell. The atmosphere in Dublin that day was electric with tension and fear. Death stalked the streets. I went to the Bridewell at once on this mission.

As those men were not known to me, Thornton gave me their description. Going from cell to cell (it is quite a small place) I examined the occupants through the peep-hole. There were only a handful of poor wretches there and not one in the least like those sought. Returning to the church, I told Thornton they were not there. He asked me where I thought they were and knowing that they had been arrested by the castle Auxies, I answered: 'Probably dead.'

I told Thornton to clear off at once. He and those with him were armed, of course. It was certain death for them if the Auxies came on the scene. When they heard me tell Thornton there was nothing doing, those men were relieved at being let off this suicide mission. So should I in like circumstances. Fifteen minutes after I'd left the Bridewell, two lorry-loads of Tans arrived to garrison the place. They would have been just in time to mow down the squad. Those men surely led charmed lives.

The castle Auxies had murdered the three suspects, putting out a story that they had attempted to disarm their guards. This took place in the Auxies' quarters, in a guard-room just inside the Palace Street castle gate. McKee, a printer by trade, was a grave loss to the Dublin Brigade as he was a very able man; the leadership following his was not the same. He was really irreplaceable.

I have read that McNamara and I reported to Collins that those men had been bayoneted and otherwise mutilated; this is not true. We never saw the bodies and certainly made no such statements; the truth was bad enough without embroidery.

No inquests were held. The British did away with them after a Cork jury had brought in a verdict of wilful murder against Lloyd George and his *confrères*. Collins mourned McKee and Clancy. Following on Bloody Sunday, as it came to be called, the British arrested thousands of suspects. Raiding went on non-stop. Those arrested were paraded before masked spotters, and in other cases prisoners were observed through slits in doors and fences.

One night at this time my contact failed to turn up outside Jervis Street Hospital; I couldn't blame him considering the terror in the air. It was a foggy winter's night. I heard a quick step approaching. It was Collins. 'What in hell did you want to come here for?' I said. 'It's terribly dangerous to be out.' He grinned. 'I couldn't find anybody else.' I was horrified that he might be captured through his desire that I should not go away disappointed. I begged of him to leave, saying that what brought me there was of no importance.

After this body-blow on Bloody Sunday there was an interval while the British sought to reorganise their network. Their star operators were gone and those now coming on the scene were not anything like as good. One Volunteer, named Frank Teeling, had been wounded and captured on Bloody Sunday. He was rescued from prison before they had time to execute him. Another man, McNamara, a red-haired shop assistant from Dun Laoghaire (which is six miles from Dublin), was identified by witnesses, or a witness, as having participated in the affair. He and others were tried by court martial in the City Hall.

The English brought over crack counsel to prosecute; afterwards rewarding some of them with the ermine.

It is, or ought to be, well known that a military court is the world's worst. It is not hard to guess why this should be. The

125

personnel, being military officers, are themselves active participants in the warfare which necessitates the court; the defendants are their enemies in the struggle—'only God can help him whose accuser is also his judge'. By his very nature, a military officer has neither the mental equipment nor training requisite to weigh evidence, even if he could be impartial. He is meeting daily and living with those, like himself, exposed to the hazards of war with the defendant's colleagues. When one adds that here the courts were composed of aliens and oppressors, with a decided superiority complex towards mere Irish, it was like appearing before the devil in the court of hell. So our red-haired friend from Dun Laoghaire had not got a dog's chance.

As has been mentioned, those officers had been shot precisely at 9 a.m. on that Sunday. However, a local policeman at his trial gave evidence that he had seen red-head at 9 a.m. Mass in Dun Laoghaire that morning. He was acquitted. (Years afterwards I was able to help out the witness when he was in great trouble.) Red-head lives in U.S.A.

Others tried were not so lucky and were executed. One of those facing trial was Moran from Co. Galway. At the time of Teeling's escape from the fortress-like prison of Kilmainham, Moran had been given the chance of escaping. He refused, saying they could not convict him. He let someone else go. He had too much faith in courts martial, was convicted and executed, on 14th March, 1921.

Hurley's case throws a light on courts martial. Amongst the most zealous of the political G-men was Tommy Oldsworth, a conscientious Loyalist Protestant. He spent most of his waking hours outside Sinn Fein H.Q. at 6 Harcourt Street, Dublin, noting the comings and goings of everyone there. One dark night, Paddy Daly, O.C. of the Active-Service Unit of the Volunteers, accompanied by his adjutant Joe Leonard, another hardy fellow, was passing along that street. They saw Tommy. Leonard was unarmed, Daly had a revolver with one round. He said to his companion, 'I won't meet Mick again without having a go at that bastard.' (Apparently Collins had been twitting him about Oldsworth.) He added: 'You run!' 'No,' replied Leonard, 'you let fly and we'll both run!' Daly fired his single round at Tommy who was a very tall broad-shouldered man. He fell. The pair took

126

British troops in Talbot Street the day Treacy and Price, the British agent, were shot.

Above: Search by British soldiers: 1920. Below: British troops raid the Sinn Fein Bank: 1920. Photos: Independent Newspapers Ltd.

to their heels. What they did not know was that Tommy had four other G-men escorting him: at that moment they were standing so close to Daly and Leonard that they could have grabbed them. But the thing happened so quickly they were taken unawares and did not fire in the crowded street. Oldsworth recovered but cleared out. The comings and going at No. 6 went unrecorded. I think the British offered a reward for information as was usual at the time. A man came forward; I think he was a Briton. He said he recognised a newspaper seller named Hurley (who stood at his pitch a few hundred yards off) as the assailant. This poor wretch was arrested immediately and tried by court martial, found guilty and received about ten years, being identified by our friend. It is said that Hurley was compensated afterwards by Collins and I hope it is true but I doubt it. He was only one of the many victims at the time.

Failing identification, suspects were generally interned. These camps held thousands of prisoners, notably one at Ballykinlar, Co. Down. Numbers of these were held on the flimsiest suspicion and many were interned for years. The Curragh Camp had a regular village. This held hundreds of internees. A fortress-like place also for prisoners was Spike Island, off Cork coast.

One day in the castle I saw Rory O'Connor being questioned by an Auxie intelligence man, in the yard. As I passed by the fellow asked me was Rory known to me. Winking at the prisoner, I said: 'Yes, I know him well. He is perfectly harmless.' 'I'm told,' he said, 'that he is a prominent Shinner.' 'Nothing of the sort, he's only an eccentric,' I answered. Rory was interned in Curragh Camp. At this time he was Director of Engineering in the I.R.A. Some time afterwards, on the quays, I was hailed by a bearded man in clerical clothes. It was Rory, newly escaped. The man who was questioning him afterwards said he had been wounded and collected a large sum in the Recorder's Court. We had no sweepstakes at the time, but the Malicious Injuries Act acted as one, and produced windfalls to those of the right colour.

The illegal parliament, or Dail, conducted courts which did nearly all the legal business. They were excellent courts, dealing out rough and ready decisions. The officers of the court were unpaid and had no interest in prolonged litigation, and got no fees, refreshers or otherwise.

Some of the Dublin police kept lodgers. An amusing incident occurred during the Truce. Police Sergeant McMahon and his wife had a lodger who was not, in their eyes, a desirable guest. One day he arrived to find his chattels bundled up in the hall. Knowing that castle police could not appear before the Sinn Fein Court, he appeared at the local one in York Street and was awarded damages against the landlord. The Sergeant appealed at once, pleaded his case before the illegal tribunal, and had the decision quashed. With truly Machiavellian reaction, the lodger reported the Sergeant to the Castle for patronising this illegal court. The affair was handled by Station Sergeant Hurley, late of the Depot, who was decidedly nervous about the whole thing He feared that between the jigs and the reels there might be a bullet in it for him. He knew me well and asked me what he should do. This Sinn Fein Court was usually held in a hall in York Street, much used for dances, whist drives and similar functions. It is about two hundred years old. I told Hurley to go there at a time when only the caretaker was present. This man was hostile to police and would not give any information. The Inspector could then report that the complainant was lying. There was no court in York Street. He followed out this scheme. No more was heard of the matter.

The illegal government had no prisons, of course, so those convicted were generally sentenced to hard labour with a poor farmer. As a rule, they served the sentence, being afraid to clear out, as they ran a good chance of being shot. Sometimes they went over to the British, getting their captors arrested. There was a phrase current at the time: 'Removed to an unknown destination.'

Very few of the uniformed police in Dublin stuck out their necks relative to political matters, but there were one or two cases. A sergeant reported to the Tans that he had seen a few armed youths lying in ambush in the suburbs. They were arrested and executed. One of them was young Flood, of a family which suffered a great deal in the struggle. The Sergeant left the country. He used good judgement thereby. Another policeman attended Mountjoy prison one day. He had been very active against the Volunteers. A voice shouted from a window calling him by name: 'Thompson, you'll be next.' He was shot soon

128

afterwards. It was a difficult time for any sort of police. They had very little sympathy from the population. A good number of the Dublin police had resigned. More of them were afraid to go home. They were between the devil and the deep sea. Plenty of them looked the other way where rebels were concerned. One or two got shot, probably by armed criminals, using the 'troubles' to cover their nefarious activities like the assassins of Vicars.

The British, even before Broy's arrest, knew well that the G-men were no longer to be trusted, and had by-passed them for a long time. Now they decided to feed them some fake information to further a little ruse of theirs. One night in the castle office, McNamara passed to me a telephone message on a police form. These messages which are circulated to all city stations are known as routes, and are concerned with crime. This one, emanating from British military H.Q., stated that a Sinn Fein suspect named Fouvargue had escaped from three intelligence officers in a car whilst *en route* to prison. It gave his description and asked that the British military be notified of his recapture.

Now if they had said that the man (who was completely unknown to both of us) had escaped from one I.O. it might have sounded reasonable enough. But to tell us that an unarmed man had escaped out of a motor-car in the presence of three presumably armed men was imposing a strain on our credulity. Both of us thought this story too good to be true.

We gave a copy of the message to Collins next day. A week later he told us that this youth, of French parentage, had been an I.R.A. company officer in the Ranelagh area. His arrest by the British and subsequent interrogation or torture had resulted in the arrest of his whole formation a few days later. He had then skipped off to London. Later he was shot by Reggie Dunne, who also shot Field Marshal Sir Henry Wilson. Dunne was accompanied in a car by another Volunteer named Joe Shanahan who told me that on their way back from the 'execution' a policeman held them up to say that their tail-light was not working. Dunne was executed in London on 16th August 1922.

In his book Colonel Winter says that Fouvargue promised to work for them, but must have made some false step. Actually the intelligence crowd made the error of trying to be too smart and so signed the death-warrant of their dupe. Winter would not admit this, of course.

At about this time, McNamara was confidential clerk to the Assistant Commissioner. And of course 'leaking' everything to Collins. His position made him a very useful agent. One day a secret letter arrived in the castle from General Tudor's office. It said that several cases had occurred of American sailors handing over arms to the Volunteers, and that 'All U.S. sailors are now suspect'. Mac gave a copy of it to Collins. The Sinn Fein Publicity Bureau published it. A strong diplomatic protest to the British Government followed from the Americans. And a furious row ensued here. Following this came an enquiry in the castle, of which Mac knew nothing. He had just returned from Glasgow escorting a runaway Auxie who had committed some offence. He told me he was to report to the Commissioner that day. Our conversation took place in the castle yard. Looking around I remarked jocosely: 'I don't see the armoured car,' referring to Broy's arrest. Waiting outside the office, I heard Mac after a few minutes coming down the stairs, whistling between his teeth as usual. 'Dismissed!' he said. The Commissioner had made no allegations at the interview—just told him he was sacked. 'Listen, Mac!' I said, 'don't go to your father's house tonight or any other night.' He said he had no money, so when that had been adjusted he went away. Auxies in mufti were seen hanging about his neighbourhood that night. He went on the run and operated with the squad. I missed him terribly; we were great friends and now I was alone in the castle. It set me wondering when my number would come up!

A Volunteer named Matt. Furlong from Wexford, while experimenting with a home-made mortar in Meath, received injuries which killed him. His dead body lay in the mortuary of the Mater Hospital in Dublin. The British believed that the dead man was Dan Breen, the Tipperary one-man column. They sent an R.I.C. sergeant named Comerford from Tipperary to Dublin to identify him. Comerford, accompanied by a Constable Fitzmaurice, called to the castle and I was ordered to accompany them to the Mater. This was on a Saturday. We saw the dead man. Comerford immediately said that it was not Breen, 'I'd

130

know his ugly mug anywhere.' As ill-luck would have it I had a contact that night with the squad and told them casually of the visit, which I regarded as of no importance. I added that I was to meet those two R.I.C. men on the quays next day at 3 p.m., simply to go for a walk about the city. While I stood waiting for them there shortly before 3, four members of the squad arrived. To my horror the leader told me that he had orders to shoot Comerford on the spot. I could see those two men approaching. I pleaded with him not to go ahead with it, but to no purpose. In a few seconds volleys were fired at the sergeant and he fell dead. Everyone ran away. That was the most terrible episode of my life.

A quarter of an hour afterwards a phone message arrived from the Inspector-General of the R.I.C. directing me to report to him at once. With him in the office were several high-ranking R.I.C. officers and Constable Fitzmaurice. After identifying myself, the I.G., a tough looking old fellow named Smith, said to me: 'Neligan, this man,' indicating Fitzmaurice, 'says you were talking to the men who shot the Sergeant.' I denied it. He asked me what I was doing there and I replied that I was waiting for a tram to go to the park. This was stupid of me, for I was at the wrong side of the street for the park tram, but fortunately nobody spotted that. He then asked me could I identify any of the killers if they were arrested and I said 'Yes'. The fact of the matter was that I knew them well. The I.G. stated that it was astonishing how the I.R.A. found out about Comerford's journey as it was kept a close secret. At this I wildly clawed at a straw. Turning to Fitzmaurice who, like myself, was in a state of shock, I said: 'Didn't you tell me that some woman at a railway station enquired where you were going?' They all turned to him. 'Yes,' he told them. 'A woman in the magazine stall at Limerick Junction asked me where we were bound for.' I was told to go. A couple of days afterwards I read in the newspaper that the British had arrested this poor girl. It grieves me to think that I brought this trouble on her innocent head.

Now these two events put Mac and myself in jeopardy. In Mac's case, the publication of that confidential letter for the sake of a little favourable publicity pointed the finger of suspicion at him and put an end to a valuable source. The British would never have been so incautious, and I am amazed that Collins was. What Comerford had done to deserve death I do not know, or if he had done anything. Identifying a dead man was certainly not an offence at all, but of course it was not for me to question the ins and outs of the matter. That was the one day I regretted my role. If for one second I thought the poor wretch would have been shot, not a word of his visit would have been mentioned. It seems likely that he was shot as a reprisal for the shooting of Sean Treacy.

Often it becomes imperative to expose an agent. Sometimes it is done deliberately, but in Mac's case it had been done, so far as I know, without any sound reason. It would be interesting to know why it was done, but it escaped my mind at the time, and I did not enquire. That was not a time for asking questions! And events crowded each day.

16

CHRISTMAS was approaching. Charley Dalton, a member of the squad, met me. He told me that Collins was going to throw a party on Christmas night at the Gresham Hotel, in the city centre. He said Collins wanted to know would I come, and also if it were safe to hold it. He was under a terrific strain all this time and was overwhelmed with work. I knew that a little relaxation for him was imperative.

Still my reply was: 'It is not safe. It is the most dangerous place in Ireland. I am not going; tell him to keep far away from it.' Collins was told this but did not heed it. In the middle of the party ten or twelve armed Auxies rushed into the private room and held up everyone, searching them. Collins kept his head and invited them to the bar for a drink, which they accepted and cleared off. Cullen told me afterwards that he thought a (named) official of the hotel gave them away. But I did not accept that for two reasons. One was that, knowing the man, I thought he would be too cowardly; secondly, if he had given them away, the Auxies would certainly have arrested and screened everyone there. I think no one gave them away—it was just a chance encounter.

It being clear to me that the British secret service had taken over, I told Collins: 'I might as well be in the Tramway office.' 'What do you propose to do, Dave?' 'I'm going to join the British secret service,' I told him. He was astounded. 'You must be mad! you'd never be able to get in.' 'I can try, can't I?' 'Begod if you did it would be wonderful.' I made an appointment for next day with him.

Next morning I applied for an interview with an official of high rank, which was granted at once. He, in friendly fashion, asked me what was bothering me. I replied that it was my desire to become a member of His Majesty's secret service. Like Collins, the man was astonished. 'What in hell put that into your head, Neligan?' Thinking of old Superintendent Purcell, I told him: 'I'm looking for more money, Sir.' (I had no idea how those men were paid except that I felt sure they were not compensated for the risks they ran!) 'If that is the case, Neligan, I'm your man,' he replied in kindly manner. I told Collins that the affair was going ahead and that progress seemed possible. He was delighted. The officer sent for me and asked was anyone else in the G Division interested in joining. To this aspect I had given some thought, and had approached another G-man named Trant who agreed to join too, so I told the man. He wrote down his name. In a few days' time both of us were told to report to the office of Mr A. Cope, C.B., one of the Assistant Under-Secretaries, and a key-man in the administration. This we did. We were ushered into a nicely furnished office in the Upper yard. It had fine fittings including a good carpet. Being used only to bare barrack rooms, I did not realise the castle held such luxury. But of course this was an important official, not a poor policeman. We were greeted by an Englishman of tidy build, suave manners, and dressed in the height of fashion. This was Mr Cope. It was said that he had started his career as a Customs officer, had somehow come under the favourable notice of Lloyd George, who promoted him rapidly. How true this is I do not know, but later developments seem to lend it colour.

We identified ourselves and Cope received us politely. I could see our police files before him on the desk. He asked me why I wanted to join the S.S. I told him the Sinn Feiners were hateful to me, had threatened me and I wanted to get my own back; besides, I needed more money. He asked my friend and he replied in somewhat similar strain. 'You both are no friends of the Shinners, clearly,' he said. Wishing us luck, he told us to resign from the police; our resignations would go through in the ordinary way and now we were to report to a certain office across the yard.

This was a place out-of-bounds to all but the military. Red-caps (military police) and sentries, all British, stood sentinel in various corners and doorways. Immense wooden structures had

134

been erected in the yard and these were partitioned into little offices. Even the ballroom was divided up to make more offices.

A red-cap directed us to one and we knocked at the door. A voice shouted, 'Come in.' A stout red-faced Briton was alone there. He was a hardy-looking fellow of about fifty with a pugnacious expression. He repelled me and scared me; if my role was ever discovered I could expect no mercy here. Still, when I got to know him he was not a bad fellow and we got on well. His name was Major Poges. This was in May 1921.

Telling us that we had been recommended as good men, he handed us a Bible and we repeated after him: 'I . . . solemnly swear by Almighty God that I will faithfully perform the duties assigned to me as a member of His Majesty's secret service: that I will obey implicitly those placed over me: that I shall never betray such service or anything connected with it even after I have left it. If I should fail to keep this oath in every particular I realise that vengeance will pursue me to the ends of the earth. So help me God.'

He told Trant to go outside. Taking up an ordnance map he told me my area would be Kingstown (now Dun Laoghaire) and that I should stay out of the city where I was too well known. I should get some job as cover. He asked me had I any ideas in that direction. 'I'm going to be an insurance agent,' I told him. 'You will receive £7 per week. It will be brought to you by a courier to whom you will give your reports. Join the I.R.A., old boy,' said the Major, 'and if you catch Collins it will be £10,000 for you. You will be No. 68. There are other agents there; if you are ever in trouble, make this sign.' There was another sign of recognition when meeting another agent, somewhat like those of Freemasons.

He told me something about secret inks: one is urine. He gave me an automatic pistol and ammunition: it was the same weapon as the G-men used, unreliable, but handy to carry in civilian clothes. He gave me a curfew pass signed by General Boyd, C.O. Dublin Command. In answer to his knock on the wooden partition another man came into the office. He was younger, foxy-faced, dapper, handsome, and had subaltern imprinted on him. He too was English. We were introduced: 'Captain Catchpole, this is 68; he is going to operate from Kingstown.' We shook

135

hands. After further conversation they told me they'd meet me on Kingstown Pier in a few days' time.

A couple of hours later I met Collins in Gay's library. He was delighted at my successful entry. 'God, that is great.' When I told him that the city was barred to me, he said he'd send one of the squad to Dun Laoghaire to keep in touch with me. This man was Dan McDonnell, about my own age, sturdy, with a heavy mop of red hair. Silent as the grave, sober and reliable, he was ideally suited to the job and stayed with me to the end.

The Major, accompanied by the Captain, turned up on the pier and we chatted. They produced a snapshot of a round-faced, clean-shaven man. 'This fellow is a prominent Shinner' (the British did not distinguish between I.R.A. and politicians); 'he calls to No. . . . on . . . Road on Tuesday evenings; he is courting the maid there. Keep an eye out for him.' I showed the snap to Dan McDonnell and he said it was of Billy Walsh, Battalion O.C. of the Dun Laoghaire Battalion. When McDonnell told him to steer clear of that house he wanted to know where the information came from, but he was not told.

Collins told me that the Major was not known to them but the Captain was. He was a military intelligence officer. Tobin and Cullen had followed him from his barracks a few times but had lost him. It is very difficult to shadow such a man. He has been in tight corners, has developed a sixth sense. He adopts many tricks of evasion, such as whipping round a corner and standing still; changing his coat or headgear, jumping on a passing bus. When one's life is at stake perceptions are sharpened until danger can be scented in the very air.

When leaving Dublin I put my old bicycle in the guard's van of the train and travelled with it. Seated there was a decent looking old man in Post Office uniform. He was in charge of mail bags being sent on the mail boat. I asked him did he know of any suitable lodgings in Kingstown (now Dun Laoghaire). He told me he lived there and would put me up. Mr Elliott and his quiet wife and family made me very comfortable. He had been married twice and they were neutral in the struggle. This suited me well. Fred, a child of the second wife, was a postman. He often cursed when he had to go on duty at 6 a.m. He wanted to join the

136

Volunteers and asked my advice. I discouraged him, not wanting any complications. A woman visitor was an ardent Sinn Fein sympathiser and often chided me with lack of patriotism.

The courier turned up with my pay. It was about £7 per week, so far as I can recollect. He asked me to sign a receipt, which was a British Army form. This he replaced in his sock. Collins had cycled to Keegan's pub opposite Blackrock College to meet me. I saw him wave to passing lorries full of Auxiliaries who waved back. He and I concocted a report for the British and laughed heartily at the contents. We said that arms were pouring into Ireland daily for the rebels; hundreds of Volunteers offered themselves for flying columns in a desire to immolate themselves on the altar of freedom. The ordinary people were prepared to fight to the last man; millions of cash were being sent from U.S.A.; the morale of the Volunteers was buoyant. I gave the courier this gem. The secret service must have needed a headache powder having read it!

The courier was a handsome young Englishman; nearly all the personnel of that service were British. His job was to keep in touch with all agents, pay them, give and receive their reports and instructions. He was well dressed in a London-cut suit. 'When you come here again,' I told him, 'wear your oldest clothes and a battered old hat. With that rig-out you have on, your fair hair and English accent, anyone would cop you a mile away.' He was a likeable fellow and I did not want to see him finished off. When we got to know each other he told me that he took this job as his money had run out and he had no prospects. A decent poor fellow, I was sorry for him.

Collins turned up at the same pub, a very quiet place then. A big man sat in the bar sipping a soft drink. Collins jumped off the old bicycle and grinned. A few minutes earlier I'd seen him waving to lorry loads of Auxies and Tommies passing by. Collins always travelled alone and never had an escort that I could see, though many stories to the contrary have been told. He called over the big man: 'Do you know this man, Dave?' 'No,' I said, 'but he looks like a policeman.' 'Yes,' he told me: 'this is Station Sergeant Sullivan, a Kerryman and a friend. I asked him here to meet you.' Sullivan was a rock of sense, very shrewd. One

SC—E*

story, perhaps, will serve to illustrate his usefulness to Collins. It happened soon after our meeting. He was on duty in the local station one night when a youth entered. He demanded to use the phone. Sullivan told him to clear off and go to a public phone. The lad got annoyed and shouted, 'I'll let you see I've authority here!' He produced a letter signed by an Auxie I.O. saying he was to be facilitated. 'Oh,' said the Sergeant. 'Why didn't you say so in the first place? Come on in.'

He gave the lad the phone, at the same time plugging in an extension allowing him to hear the mystery man. The following conversation ensued: 'This is No. 89 from Kingstown. There are two men with guns in the Pavilion picture-house.' The youth, Graham, was an attendant there and working for the British. He was shot. Like those agents who gave their addresses to the police on night-duty, the British put too much faith in the police. Their early training, of course, taught them that the Bobby is the last word in reliability, but that does not follow outside their own homeland, least of all in a subjugated country.

I begged of Collins not to come out to Keegan's any more, being terrified that unwittingly I might be the cause of his capture. Without his help, therefore, I used to concoct those weekly reports much on the same lines as those with the dastardly outrage ending. The Major complimented me. He said that they were excellent. Always confined to generalities, never mentioning an individual, they naturally threw doubt on the ability of the British to defeat what was really a revolution. They must have been sad reading for my British masters. According to me, organised labour was wholeheartedly Sinn Fein; so were the Catholic clergy with the sole exception of Father Bended whose sermons were copied by the Tans and plastered on the dead walls—him I described as a loyal citizen.

A senior man visited me. Apropos of supplies of small arms to the I.R.A. he said: 'We are helping them out!' I enquired his meaning. 'Well, we are dropping ammunition where they'll find it. It is filled with a charge which goes off prematurely and will blow them to hell. Cartridges so marked have ZZ on the rim.' Collins, on being told, issued a warning. Col. Dan Stapleton, a Volunteer ballistics expert and chemist states that a number of rounds of

138

small arms ammunition were sent to him in 1920 for examination. This stuff emanated from a Tipperary military barracks and some had exploded, injuring a Volunteer. Dan found that 'instead of the usual propellant charge they contained guncotton in the centre of which was a tiny capsule of Fulminate of Mercury which acted as a booster to the guncotton and ensured its explosion'.

One day as I sat on the front reading a daily paper which supported the Castle regime, an elderly man greeted me. When we had exchanged remarks about the weather he went on: 'There was an ambush in Blackrock the other day—I thought the boys were trapped.' 'Are you in sympathy with them then?' I asked. 'Yes, I'd like to see every Tan in the country shot.' Such candour in those days amazed me, as nobody but a madman discussed such things with a stranger. The old man invited me to his digs for a drink on Sunday. I could bring a friend. Inquisitive to know who my friend was, and what was his name, I asked Dan McDonnell to come with me. We had a pleasant time with the old chap. On my suggestion Dan had him followed in to town the next morning. He got off at the stop nearest to Beggars Bush Barracks, an Auxie H.Q., and entered after showing his pass to a sentry. It turned out that he was a cook there but not a spy. The next place I saw him was in a tent telling fortunes!

At the time I'd joined the secret service, a colleague named Trant joined with me, being an innocent fellow whom I had persuaded to do so. When Collins heard of his joining, he said he should be shot, but I was determined that no harm should come to him—one Sergeant Comerford was enough—so I explained to Collins that he would never have thought of it but for me; that he was quite harmless and unlikely to stay in it long. This came to pass and he was fired out after a short time and rejoined the police. He must have been a poor writer of fairy-tales! Curiously enough I've never seen him from that day to this, nor did I enquire why he severed his connection with the service. We shall encounter him once again though.

The British had thought of many schemes for getting information about the rebels. One was that a letter could be dropped into any letter-box and would find its way to a post office in London specially ear-marked to receive it. Notices to this effect were published by the Castle in all the newspapers on 15th September 1920. This gave rise to frequent raids by the I.R.A. on mail bags. The Irish Post Office was certainly one of Collins' most useful services. Nothing there was hidden from him or from his agents. Nearly all the rank and file were ardent sympathisers and everyone knows the inquisitive village postmistress. She is interested in everything passing to and fro and little escapes her.

A Corkman named Pat Moynihan was a sorter in Dublin and a Sinn Fein sympathiser. One of his jobs was to sort the Castle mails which were the subject of extraordinary safeguarding precautions. The poor British Tommies whose job it was to escort them from the sorting office to the castle were very chummy with Moynihan and often offered him a lift in their armoured car. He accepted it one day. With him was a suitcase which contained the much-guarded Castle mails. He got off just outside the castle. As he told it, by sleight-of-hand he had substituted a bag full of old papers for the Government bag. Another day armed men took the Castle mails in a hold-up. Consternation reigned in the castle. I've never seen such panic. A thousand houses in Dublin were searched that day and for a week following. The raids went on day and night. They discovered nothing. Moynihan was not suspected. The Tommies were dumb of course about their breach of regulations and certainly did not suspect the cheerful Pat. To this day, I've never discovered what was in those bags or if they contained any earth-shaking revelations. I suspect that it was not worth the energy wasted, but it was great fun at the time.

The British controlled all telegraph agencies and other news media to the outside world, so their version of the news was of course one-sided, partial. Many of the correspondents were secret-service men and still are.

The biggest news agency was run by descendants of a naturalised German, now more British than themselves, as anyone interested can find out. So the struggle here was presented to the world as a handful of crazy Irishmen inexplicably in rebellion against their benevolent British fathers. The 'Irish Problem', for centuries the plaything, the shuttlecock of Imperial politics, again held the stage. Gladstone's effort to give Home Rule fell flat; so did Asquith's. Now the gun was the arbiter.

The courier brought me an anonymous letter addressed to the Castle. It bore a Foxrock postmark and said that a red-haired I.R.A. man frequented the railway station there. He had wrung the necks of some military homing-pigeons on their way to an outpost. I was directed to go there and see if such was the case. Needless to say I had no intention of cramping the red-haired man's plans. Yet, never having set foot in Foxrock, I must go so that something of the lay-out would be known to me, if questioned. So on a fine sunny afternoon I cycled a few miles south of Dun Laoghaire.

Foxrock was then a pleasant, quiet country place with a few nice houses and Leopardstown racecourse nearby. When I arrived no one was in the station but the stationmaster and an old porter. As I gaped at the scenery, a well-dressed lad of about ten came through the little gate on to the platform and looked me up and down. He went away after this survey, but immediately returned and had another look. 'What in hell is that kid up to?' I asked myself. An uneasy feeling possessed me. Seeing a train coming towards Dublin I decided to clear off. A dozen men dashed into the station in civilian clothes. Each had a ·45 revolver with a holster and had a lanyard about his neck, military fashion. A red-haired man led them. Pointing their weapons at me, they brought me to an old garage owned by Mr Tracey, down a lane. I was questioned as to my identity and business. They made no effort to search me. When leaving Dun Laoghaire that morning I had imagined that this red-haired man was a myth, so I had in my pockets the anonymous letter, a ·38 pistol and a curfew pass. These were all sure passports to a better world when found by a flying column which now confronted me. So when they asked me to prove that I was an insurance agent, I told them that if they allowed me to put my hand in my pocket I'd show them. The leader agreed. So fishing carefully to leave the curfew pass, the pistol and the anonymous letter behind, I produced some blank insurance papers which satisfied him. If those men had found those papers I was as good as dead. They told me to go away. They didn't have to repeat it! The old bike flew down the road before they had a chance to recall me. I told Collins about the affair and he arranged for me to meet the I.O. for that area,

Bobby Keane from Blackrock, so never again did this bother me.

Of course I had not reported to the British of my encounter with the column. There was a danger that some busybody, or the author of the anonymous letter might have seen it and reported to the Castle. Then I should be in the soup. I told them the red-haired man was not to be seen.

The courier brought along a colleague who lodged with him. He too was English, young, heavily built, placid-looking. His principal interests were food and wine, of which he was an excellent judge. Billiards likewise fascinated him. I used to spend hours watching them play. They invited me to their digs in the house of a loyalist professional man where they played the piano and sang when they were not making eyes at the landlady's fair daughter. They were amateur actors and good fun.

In a report, I'd pointed out that it was an error to keep agents in watertight compartments; we should be allowed to meet and compare notes. My British masters approved and directed me to come into town one day. We were to meet at the North Dublin Union. This was an old work-house building now serving half as a military barrack and half as an Auxie H.Q.

I found myself facing about twenty-five men in a room with distempered walls and a baize-covered table. The Captain introduced us district by district. The Kingstown group consisted of an Englishman, another Irishman and myself.

The Briton was a hard-bitten old ex-sergeant-major, an old sweat who had spent years in the cavalry. He was over fifty, a little gnarled fellow. He invited me to his flat. His nice Irish wife, a soldier's daughter, used to upbraid me for working for the British while the old sweat sat there smiling like a Cheshire cat. I used to reply: 'I'm working for them but you're worse—you married one.' In spite of divided allegiance they hit it off very well. The Irishman was an ex-clerical student still wearing the dark suit and a T.T. badge. He soon cleared out. The only other Irishman in that room was an ex-tea-planter from the East, who came home in ill-health. He was a decent sort of fellow but melancholic and morose. He often invited me to his house where his quiet-mannered, neat wife made tea. The poor devil probably took this job because he could find nothing else; I pitied both of them.

At the North Dublin Union we had had a lively discussion about our operations. The ex-Sergeant-Major said it was very difficult for an Englishman. First of all he found it necessary to look for lodgings and his accent, even his clothes, gave him away immediately. Thus he had to put up in the house of a Loyalist (i.e. pro-British) who could give no help and did not know what was going on, or maybe was afraid. This of course was perfectly true and also not easily remedied!

The Major addressed us and gave us a pep-talk. Everything was going well; the gunmen were on the run (which certainly was a fact, in a sense); another year would finish them; we should keep right after them and undermine their conspiracy. The old sweat whispered to me: 'He's living in barracks, not like us.' It was so. This man, with fire in his belly, slept behind tramping sentries and barbed wire. The Captain used to boost him to me, saying he'd spent years in an old tenement in a back street in Dublin, but I spoiled the effect by asking where he lived now. Both of them lived in barracks. As they say in Co. Clare: only a step-mother would blame them!

Several of those Englishmen (not the Major or Captain) used to say to me: 'By God, Neligan, if I were an Irishman and an R.C. I'd be a Sinn Feiner too!' And this was no trap, they really meant it. The sporting Englishman, at his best!

Dan McDonnell told me that the local Volunteers were going to chain up a robber to the church gates in Dun Laoghaire on the next Sunday. I asked him to have this transferred to Dalkey. He came back and told me this would be done. The British were very anxious to shoot up the Volunteer escort—they didn't care a damn about the robber. As the rebels had no prisons, they hit on this idea of punishment; it was a variation of being put in the stocks. The victim had a placard with details of his offence: a public punishment now adopted in China! I reported to the British that rebels would chain a man to Dun Laoghaire Church next Sunday and went along myself. The Major and Captain turned up with a big squad armed to the teeth but the quarry did not appear. Next day the newspapers reported guardedly that a man had been chained up in Dalkey. (They had to keep one eye on the censor.) The Major came out. 'By God, Neligan, that was good information! The blighters changed the venue at the last moment!' I thought the moment propitious to ask for a raise. The British agents were better paid. He wanted to know how I'd discovered that, but got an evasive reply. He granted it. Shades of Superintendent Purcell!

The Captain arrived one day driving an old taxi, suitable for a dear old dowager. He kept it in a city garage owned by a Loyalist. He used to attend the mail boat with it regularly; perhaps he imagined that some courier would arrive and demand to be brought to Collins' H.Q. To this day I cannot fathom of what earthly use was that old wagon, except that we got a few jaunts in it. True enough, an alleged American reporter came off the boat one day and was met by the old bus, as he was an agent. In next to no time he sought an interview with Collins, but did not get it as I'd warned him. After the war was over, the garage man got the O.B.E. for his pains! He cleared out of here hurriedly but no one had anything against him. He was only interested in earning a few pounds. Every time I pass that garage I think of the ancient sedan and wonder where it finished its career.

Catchpole had served in India. His conversation was interlarded with such expressions as pukka, gun-wallah, gharry (an outside car). He used a share of London thieves' argot too: rumble = suspect; grass = informer; crib = house. A likeable fellow, he regarded his duty as a job of work, and did not engage in any high-falutin' sentiments, unlike some of our bombasts.

The courier was going home on leave. He brought his successor. This was a Welshman, young, with a cast in one eye. He was courting a Dublin girl and often went to Mass with her, though not a Catholic. He was a harmless poor wretch. The other courier returned. He told me that he was in danger of being sacked unless he turned up some information about the rebels. He begged me to help him! In my time at the castle, I knew a civilian named McIntosh. A great hulking bruiser, he used to go raiding and drinking with the Auxies. A rich man, he only wanted to pose as a big gunman. I'd never bothered to tell anyone of his mixing with the Auxies—if I had he would have come to a speedy end. How-

144

ever, when the Englishman asked my help, it struck me that I should bring him along to McIntosh who was a Freemason and Loyalist. We should see what game he was playing, besides swash-buckling. Next day we visited him at his office. Of course he knew me as a G-man. He hailed us: 'Where have you been this long time, Neligan?' 'Listen, Mac,' I said, 'this is one of your Castle friends. He wants information about the Shinners.' Mac turned the colour of death. Looking around fearfully, he whis-pered: 'No, by God. No! Did you know Cariot?' 'No,' I said, 'who is he?' 'He was a pal of mine; we were always together. One day he was sitting on the sea-wall at Clontarf. A fellow cycled up and shot him. By God that finished me with that crowd.' Cariot was the son of a Dublin legal man, had no occupation, and was working secretly for the Auxies. After his death, his poor old father offered a reward to anyone who would come forward and prove that he was a spy. There were no takers.

Our next visit was to an Orangeman who promised to do everything he could. I arranged with the courier to let me see his information. As everybody knew his form, I was not afraid that he would do any harm, and did not even bother to tell Collins. He never gave any information. When we left Mac's office, the courier, visibly shaken, said to me: 'I must be a bloody fool! There's an Irishman shaking with fear. I am a silly clot, coming over here sticking my nose into this bloody business. To hell with it!'

One day the landlord's son Fred McAllister told me I was wanted at the door. Outside I found representatives of both sides—Dan McDonnell and the courier. I introduced them and we went off and had tea together—Dan was supposed to be my insurance inspector.

Another day we went to Greystones, a pleasant resort in Co. Wicklow. With me were two English agents. The first person I saw in the lounge was Collins, having tea. I introduced him to those men; then he beckoned me outside for a chat. While we were talking, out of the corner of my eye I saw the manageress, Miss McDermott, a very stout woman, frantically signalling Collins. He went out to her and she said, 'For the love of God, keep away from that fellow Neligan, he's always here with British officers!' Collins told her not to worry. While he was out one of the agents said to me, 'He's a fine fellow! Would he help us?' I explained that as he was known to be hostile to the rebels he would not be able to give any information. Collins used to go to Greystones visiting De Valera's wife and family, though he was the time overwhelmed with work. He never neglected his friends.

He had a series of rooms or offices about the city, which he called joints. One day I saw him emerge from the shop of a Jewish jeweller. He had an office overhead. Most of those were found by Mr Noyk, a Jewish solicitor and faithful friend of Collins and Griffith and of mine. A Jew was about the last man to be suspected of rebel sympathies by the Castle, and so Noyk did much useful work. Openly he defended various prisoners before courts martial and so did Sean O'hUadhaigh whom the Auxies carted about as a hostage. Of course in those offices Collins posed as a business man, and the landlord never suspected the sort of business he was engaged in. Batt O'Connor, a Kerry bricklayer and builder, constructed several secret chambers for Collins, one in his own house. Though I've never seen them, it is said that they were undetectable, like the priest's hole in the time of another terror. These secret joints were known to only a few of his intimates. (It was better not to know them, in case of torture.)

In mid-city Mary Street, Collins had a secret office. One day he was lunching with O'Sullivan, the Adjutant-General of the Volunteers. Suddenly, apropos of nothing, he said: 'There's something wrong at Mary Street. I'm not going back there!' That sixth sense! He kept regular hours and used to go back there every day at 2 p.m. That particular day a crowd of Auxies entered shortly before 2, and waited. All they got was his fountain pen, and the personal effects of a poor major* who had been shot in Co. Cork. Collins proposed returning them to his widow with a touching letter of farewell from her husband. This raid smelled of treachery and was certainly no fluke. Especially as, some days earlier, they had raided next door to another secret office. That time Joe O'Reilly, diving through a skylight, had dangled from a

* Major Compton Smith, D.S.O., was executed by the I.R.A. on 28th April 1921, following on General Strickland's refusal to exchange him for six volunteers executed in Cork on that day.

roof-beam over the heads of terrified sempstresses. We never discovered the source of this information, but those were really close shaves. It looked as if someone had betrayed him. It shook him at the time.

So many worked for the British that it was impossible to counter all. He had another desperately close call at the home of Miss Patricia Hoey, a journalist. Miss Hoey's mother, an aged lady, lived with her. She persuaded the raiding Auxies who awaited Collins' coming (he had a secret office there) that her old mother was in danger of death. They escorted her to the home of a woman doctor, Dr Lynn, who just in time conveyed a warning to Collins to keep away. The doctor, who did not know the Hoeys, was an ardent Sinn Fein sympathiser.

One day Dan McDonnell and I saw a terrific pall of smoke over the city. 'That's the Custom House,' said Dan, 'it was to be burned today.' And so it was. The British had early warning from a Civil Servant, an Irishman, who phoned Inspector McCabe, who passed it on to the Castle. The Volunteers had neglected to cut one phone. Though the huge and lovely building was destroyed, it was an expensive operation for the Dublin Brigade.

Owing to the early warning, the Auxies and great number of Tommies surrounded the place, shot up a few outposts, and captured a great number of the sabotage squad. Any man whose clothing smelled of petrol or paraffin was immediately bundled into a lorry. My brother Sean came home on leave from seavoyaging. His uniform impressed the S.S. men to whom I introduced him; they thought he was in the Navy, high in prestige at home. The Scots skipper of his ship reported him to Scotland Yard as a Sinn Feiner.

The Auxies planned foot-patrols to catch the Volunteer bombing squads then active, but I conveyed a warning in time. I met Collins; we had not met for several months. He looked heavier, older, and had a pallor. His appearance shocked me. 'Any news, Dave?' 'Yes, Cope met De Valera in town last night,' I answered. 'How the hell did you hear that?' I laughed. 'Walls have eyes and ears.' The information came from a source close to Cope. 'Yes,' said Collins, 'there's a peace move on, but it is supposed to be a dead secret.'

One day Dan McDonnell told me that the Auxies were to be shot up in Grafton Street vicinity. They used to frequent the cafés and bars about there and could easily be picked out in their loud suits and jaunty ties. Besides, the squad now had photographs of F Company. The job was called off.

Tom Ennis was in charge of the Custom House job. He was a tiny fellow but there was nothing tiny about his courage. That day he was one of the last to leave the burning building. With two comrades he peeped through a corrugated-iron gate. He saw serried rows of soldiers and Auxies lying prone with machine-guns trained on the building. Armoured cars with Vickers guns ready to fire stood in the streets. Turning to his friends he said: 'Boys, we may say our prayers.' Behind their backs was a sea of flames; the files of the bureaucrats were well alight. Soon the building would be only a shell. Drawing their Peter-the-painter (Mauser) pistols, Ennis and his comrades opened the gate and dashed into the middle of the cordon. This apparition so startled the British that for a moment they did not fire. Ennis was nearly around the corner before a machine-gun opened up on him, shattering one of his legs. As the gunner was lying prone the traversing fire was a bit low. Incredible as it sounds, Ennis grabbed the shattered leg and hopped around the corner. A covered railway van was standing there. The driver, who was not even a Volunteer, took in the situation at a glance, seized Ennis and flung him under a tarpaulin, whipped up his horse and cleared off. His comrades were wounded and captured.

Pat Moylett, a native of the West of Ireland lives in Dublin now. He is eighty-six years old, hale and hearty. Pat would really require a book to himself and maybe I'll write it yet.

In his youth Moylett went to London to work. A fellow of infinite charm and sterling honesty, he soon made good in business and made a lot of money. He made friends in very influential British political circles, no mean feat then for an Irishman. When the revolution started up, he tried many times to mediate with Lloyd George and other influential politicians and the 'Thunderer' (*The Times*) paid him a tribute, in a sub-leader which I've read.

At this time he had a prosperous business in the West of

148

Ireland. The Tans seized his house and everything he had and ordered him out of the town. He went on the run. He was a bibliophil and had some very rare books. The raiders on one occasion walked off with his copy of Audubon's *The Birds of America*. He never saw it again. This book is worth its weight in gold now. Moylett never received any credit or compensation for the damage done to him or for his work and neither did he look for it.

Lloyd George wanted the I.R.A. to surrender their arms and excluded Collins and Mulcahy from negotiations. When he received a telegram from an Irish crackpot asking 'what peace steps do you propose' he was cock-ahoop and said he had 'murder by the throat'. He soon changed his tune though.

McKeon, a famous column leader, was under sentence of death and Lloyd George wanted to exclude him from amnesty but quickly forgot about it when he received a report from General McCready that the troops in Ireland were exhausted. One should have a certain amount of sympathy for the General, who had a terrific problem on his hands.

17

A TRUCE was declared on the 11th July 1921. The courier arrived with instructions that it made no difference; we were to carry on as before, taking precautions against discovery. The paymaster was going on leave and I was directed to take over, paying the agents weekly. The Volunteers slacked off. Some got too big for their boots and could not be bothered keeping appointments, but wasted their time showing off and swaggering about.

Trant had rejoined the police, as I have said, and one day after the truce stood in the street waiting for his girl friend. He was not aware that he was outside the secret H.Q. of the Dublin Volunteers Brigade. As they knew of his joining the secret service and had not heard of his resignation, naturally they concluded he was watching them. He was arrested and conveyed to a camp called Mount Seskin in the Wicklow Mountains. Dan McDonnell told me of this wonderful capture; they wanted me to go up to identify him. 'Tell them to go to hell. That man is harmless and should be released at once,' I told Dan. They let him go, but as he had been absent for two days he was hauled before the Commissioner. This cost him £2, as that officer described the account of his misadventure as a ridiculous lie.

I was ordered in to the castle where I was directed to the office of Count Sévigné, the head of the British secret service. He was a little pale-faced fellow with sharp features, bright eyes and good manners. He wrote my description on a writing-pad: 'About 6 ft. 1 in., 22 years old, long face, clean shaven.' (This was for the benefit of the man who was to meet me.) He gave me a sealed letter and told me I was to go to London next day. I would be met in Holyhead and get further directions.

150

Collins was going to London at this time (October 1921), against his will, to take part in peace negotiations with Lloyd George's government. I visited several 'joints' looking for a contact but drew blank. There was nothing for it but to go to the Liaison Office at the Gresham Hotel. Emmet Dalton, whom I knew, was the Volunteer Liaison Officer. Having had a good look around, I darted up the stairs and stood outside the door marked Liaison Officer.

Hearing an English voice I thought, 'that is Cope'. He seemed to be saying 'good-bye'. I dived into an empty bedroom just as Dalton's door opened and Cope went down the stairs. Slipping into Dalton's office, I startled him. 'Where in hell did you come out of—did you see Cope?' 'Yes, but he did not see me. Listen, Emmet, I'm going to London tomorrow, and here is a letter the British gave me. We'll have to get it opened.'

Dalton left immediately and made an appointment for me. I cleared off. The letter was returned in a few hours. Pat Moynihan, a P.O. official whose hobby was other people's letters, had done a wonderful job on the seal. He could have saved himself the trouble as the letter was in cipher. There was neither time nor facility for deciphering it.

When Collins heard of my trip he sent two members of the squad to shadow me; these were Bob O'Neill and Paddy Kennedy. At Holyhead a woman with hennaed hair turned up and gave me a letter which began: 'Dear Neligan', and directed me to a London hotel. There I met an agent, English, who kept in touch with me every day and showed me the sights. Feminine companionship was proffered me but declined! As he knew the place well and was congenial company, I enjoyed it well enough, but I was under a strain as day followed day without any further instructions reaching me. Nearly every night I used to meet Liam Tobin or Dolan for a chat.

One of the sights of London in the winter of 1921 was the number of ex-officers begging in the streets. Some of the poor devils played barrel-organs to which they had pinned their decorations. Legions of them stood in the gutter selling toys and matches, having been demobbed with a few pounds. It was pitiable. No wonder they'd joined the Auxies. Lloyd George's slogan that he'd make it a land fit for heroes was just a politician's glib propaganda.

At last I received a telegram from Dublin recalling me. Going to Euston that afternoon I saw an immense throng cheering and laughing. I asked a Bobby what was on and he replied: 'It's them Shinners, y'know, they say there's peace with 'em.'

As I made my way to the train I saw the delegation—Griffith, Collins, Barton, Childers and Duggan. On the boat I saw Cope, Collins and Tobin. When Collins saw me he signalled to Tobin to come out. We discussed the settlement. Tobin said: 'We'll have to face our die-hards now,' the first time I'd heard the expression used in Irish politics. We were to hear it often enough afterwards!

On my return I met the Major. He did not know (or professed not to know) the object of my journey. Whatever it was, the signing of the Treaty in December 1921 put an end to it. It has remained a mystery to this day. The Major discussed the settlement with me. He thought the British Government had 'surrendered to murder'. High-ranking British military were nearly all Tory in politics and of course took their cue from General McCready. This officer, who had in his final reports to the British Government stated that his troops were in the last stages of exhaustion, no doubt gave expression to bellicose remarks to his colleagues. The Major also thought that the Irish would be 'at one another's throats in a few months'. I put this down to another English libel at the time.

If the Treaty was not passed, he said: 'we will flood the place with troops'. This was mere bluff, because we knew they had not got them. The great majority of soldiers (other ranks) who had gone through the First War had left the army, being heartily sick of soldiering. In fact it was a good job for the Volunteers that they had to face only poor young raw conscripts, for that is what most of them were. After all it was the rank and file who 'carried the can' as they say themselves.

The Treaty debate went on endlessly in secret sessions of the Dail. Curfew had ended and people breathed freely again. It was no longer dangerous to walk in the streets—no volleys crashed out, no grenades burst.

The Treaty was ratified by a majority of seven. The Auxies in

152

the castle, warned of disbandment, mutinied, demanding jobs, gratuities and pensions.

I was ordered in to the castle to pick out the ringleaders, which was soon done. The British Government threw in the sponge. The Auxies and Tans got twelve years added to their service in order to qualify them for pensions and were offered jobs in the Palestine police, then a British responsibility.

The British secret service prepared to wind up; we were put on half-pay. When Collins heard this he volunteered to make it up for me. This was the first time I had accepted money from him or from Sinn Fein.

I was in the castle with the Major and some others the day Collins and Griffith arrived to take it over. The Bastille, which had been England's since the time of King John, now was owned by the Irish people. A crowd gathered. Old foxy-face, the Chief Superintendent, shouted, 'Up Sinn Fein.' The old Major smiled: 'The King is dead, long live the King.'

Each secret agent received with his last pay a circular letter from General H. H. Tudor thanking him for 'his magnificent services in Ireland'.

Collins and Griffith set up a Provisional Government with the support of the pro-Treaty members of the Dail. They took over Oriel House, an old red-brick building near Westland Row and Trinity College. In it was the nucleus of a detective force and intelligence unit. Broy, McNamara and I were sent there. Tobin, Cullen and Thornton were there also, with some picked intelligence men from the Dublin Brigade.

Demobilised Auxies were staying in Dublin hotels, notably in the Hotel Russell, at that time owned by Count Sévigné's mother-in-law. A few of us were sent from Oriel House to arrest them, as it was feared they would commit robberies. We rounded up six or eight of them. Sévigné appeared and asked me where we were bringing them. I told him I knew nothing about it. We conveyed them to the Bridewell, which I had searched for McKee. One drew a gun but I took it away from him; he perhaps thought he was going to be bumped off. The British raised the matter with Collins; the Auxies were released on condition that they left the country. They cleared off.

Cope sent for me. I went to his office. 'Tell me, Neligan, aren't you one of our fellows?' 'Yes, Sir.' 'I'm told you're working for the Provisional Government. How the hell did you get in with them?' 'I'll tell you, Sir. There was a meeting of resigned and dismissed police in the Mansion House. [There was, right enough; I'd read about it in the newspapers.] Those fellows asked for their pensions. A spokesman from the Provisional Government told them that they would not give them pensions, but that if they wanted employment to apply to Oriel House. So I applied and got in.' Cope slapped his thigh. 'By Jove! If Collins only knew! Have you a rank there?' 'No, Sir. We all had the same pay.'

Having got rid of these preliminaries, the real purpose of the interview appeared. 'Tell me, Neligan, is Collins in earnest about the Treaty?' I had not laid eyes on Collins since the night on the mail boat, and had no idea how he felt about the present situation. Of course, knowing the man, I was well aware that having signed it he was not going to back out of it. These thoughts passed rapidly through my mind. I answered, 'He is, Sir.' The next question was: 'Will there be a fight?' This is where I wanted a crystal ball, or access to Biddy Early, an old Clare woman credited with foretelling. Years afterwards, a local man showed me her back-garden burial place.

At the time of my interview with Cope the split in the I.R.A. was plain to see, but no fighting had occurred, though the situation was explosive. I answered Cope: 'Yes.' 'Who is going to win that fight, Neligan?' was his next poser. Any kind of war is utterly unpredictable as is well known. This applies to civil war above all. I had no idea who would win, and fervently I hoped that wiser counsels would prevail, but I answered: 'Collins will.' 'Why do you say that?' 'Well, he is the ablest man they have and has the toughest men in the I.R.A. with him.' Though it was true that some tough men were pro-Treaty, people like Liam Lynch were not. 'I'm damned glad to hear you say that, Neligan. I'm leaving here soon. I think the Treaty is a good thing for Ireland. I'll be able to tell the British Government what you've told me.' 'Yes, Mr Cope, you are leaving here but I'm staying here; what reward do I get for risking my life in the British secret service?' 'Don't say another word, old boy, I'll fix up your pension.'

154

This was one of Cope's last official acts; he had me transferred to the R.I.C., added twelve years to my service, and saw that I was granted the sum of £65 per annum. I should have joined the fellows with the barrel-organs!

When Liam Tobin heard I'd been given a British pension he nearly passed out. As an alternative to a pension, Cope said I could go to India in the British service. I wrote to Collins telling him of this and of the interview with Cope. He replied that I was not to go away. There was a clause abating the pension if I served in any police force. The magnanimous British, when they knew the whole story, did nothing about it. Unlike us, when a fight is over they are prepared to let bygones be bygones.

Once again I met Cope. He came to Oriel House one day to tell us that his motor-car had been seized by armed men as he travelled through the city with McAllister, Assistant Liaison Officer. We sent out a squad who happened to come on the stolen car and promptly wounded the driver, who crashed into the railings of Baggot Street Hospital, conveniently enough. The car was left in Oriel House and afterwards raffled by Joe O'Reilly. It was a huge, six cylinder, open saloon which was a terrible swallower of petrol.

When the British were leaving here, Collins tried to get them to leave their secret contemporary records behind but they refused. They burned many of them in the castle. The residue they packed securely for transfer. That day Collins mobilised the squad, the Active Service Unit and elements of the Dublin Brigade, to seize the papers. The British were taking no chances though. At least half-a-dozen armoured cars escorted them to the North Wall, with lorries of troops. Following out their policy of protecting their sources. The archives must now be gathering dust in some corner of England, if Hitler's blitz did not do away with them.

The Civil War which followed the Treaty dragged on for a couple of years after the death of Collins but the bitterness engendered lasts still to some extent. I shall say no more about that. The anti-Treaty party was beaten but is now in power (1967).

Those described as Loyalists and Protestants turned out the most law-abiding citizens we have and Cosgrave's Government was fully supported by them. Their fears that Home Rule would equate Rome Rule were not borne out: on the other hand every native administration has acted with commendable justice and toleration towards this minority. An early Governor-General was the Protestant Gaelic Leaguer and Scholar, Dr Douglas Hyde. He lived to a great age, like Tim Healy, also Governor-General of the Free State.

Ernest Blythe, a non-Catholic, was Minister for Finance in Cosgrave's Government for the years 1923–32. Frugal Blythe kept down the National Debt. It has now reached astronomical proportions and will be a real pain in the neck for future governments.

The squad, which was a whole-time unit, numbered a dozen or fifteen. They were picked men and were all on the run from enemy forces. Each received a pittance from Collins to pay his expenses. Tobin and Cullen I have described. Others known to me were Tom Kehoe, from Wicklow, a poor shop-assistant. A fine-looking fellow in his twenties, he possessed glowing enthusiasm, a light heart and icy courage. He was to die in the Civil War. Another was Charley Byrne, a Dublin man whom they called the Count for his cheerful mien, bright manner and good humour in every situation. He was another of outstanding courage and devotion. Jimmy Slattery, a tiny Clareman with one hand who handled every situation with aplomb. Ned Kelliher, a silent Dublinman who could always be relied on. Joe Dolan, a little foreign-looking Dublinman who went about with a ·45 revolver in his pocket and was 'quick on the draw'. In his lapel he wore a British Army badge enscribed: 'For King & Country' and he had entwined it with red, white and blue ribbon. When the Tans and Tommies saw it they passed Dolan through the cordons murmuring: 'one of our fellows'. Joe McGuinness, Jim McGuinness, V. Byrne, Ben Byrne, M. McDonnell were active squad men.

Frank Saurin was a Dublinman and perhaps the best-dressed Volunteer. He was so impeccably turned out with a nice suit and lavender gloves that the enemy thought he was too respectable looking to be a belligerent. Consequently, he frequently sauntered through cordons and search-parties unhindered, though often

156

armed and carrying dangerous papers. He is dead. All the others are, I am glad to say, alive, except McDonnell who died in the U.S.A.

Charley Dalton, a native of Dublin, though only a boy, rendered excellent service and so later did his brother Emmet.

Pat McCrea, a Wicklow man (now dead), was an expert driver, who once drove an armoured car into Mountjoy in a vain endeavour to rescue Sean McKeon, who had been arrested in March 1920. The Tommy driver from whom it was taken remarked afterwards: 'That bloody car was giving me trouble all that week, yet a Goddam Paddy sat in and went off like a bullet in it.'

Bob O'Neill, a Clareman, and Paddy Kennedy from Tipperary were utterly reliable and cheerful companions. Billy Stapleton from Dublin was a pal of Jimmy Conroy, the one-man column. When those two travelled together it was wigs on the green! Both are still to the good. Long afterwards it fell to my lot to verify Conroy's application for a military pension. He had set out an account of the operations he had carried out. It covered many pages and gave a blow-by-blow account of one man's war effort. It was scarcely credible. As I read this thriller I could not repress a smile. Conroy was present and thought this was cynicism or unbelief on my part. 'It's all true too Dave,' he said, 'strange as it may seem.' If ever anyone deserved a pension, it was he.

Without the squad and the Active Service Unit the revolution in the city of Dublin would have fallen flat.

Paddy Daly and Joe Leonard were active leaders and well they carried out all tasks assigned to them. They are both dead now. Dublin men both, Daly was a carpenter by trade. Like Thornton, Tobin and Cullen, he had fought in 1916 and was a regular daredevil. Of active build and cheerful outlook, he was always ready for a scrap backed up by Leonard with his hearty laugh and childlike simplicity of manner. All those fellows, without a shadow of exaggeration, were of heroic mould and truly formidable soldiers. Jim Dempsey, also from the city, a battalion officer, was like Daly an old I.R.B. man and had fought in 1916. Of gigantic strength, he was often called on for dangerous assignments and never failed. On the run, he was picked up by British forces after Bloody Sunday on his first flying visit home to his old mother but was released for want of proof. There the British missed one of their most redoubtable foes. He lost an eye in the Civil War and now lives in Kerry, cheerful as ever. His Dublin accent, though, has now superimposed on it a Kerry twang.

Brugha, the Dail Minister for Defence, and Collins had at their call several Volunteer organisers on a roving commission to ginger up activities. The most prominent of those were Sean McBride, a son of the executed 1916 leader; Ernie O'Malley, who wrote a good book on the struggle, *On another man's wound* (London 1936); Peader McMahon, later Chief of Staff of the State Army; Sean Kavanagh, later Prison Governor, a Dublin man; and Paddy Colgan, from Maynooth, Co. Kildare. All of those men had hair-breadth escapes and lived truly adventurous lives. The British issued from the Castle a propaganda newspaper for the Tans. This used to say: 'Co. Kildare is quiet' or 'no activity in Co. Mayo'. On reading this Collins used to say: 'Send for Ernie O'Malley, McBride or one of the others.' Whoever was available was despatched immediately to the quiet front and soon after things began to hum there. They often shot it out with enemy parties and sometimes found it impossible to find lodgings, for any one found harbouring them was liable to sudden death. Professor Hayes, a Senator and scholarly Dublin man, tells me that at the height of the terror, only fifteen or twenty householders in Dublin were willing to hide Mulcahy, Collins or other wanted men, and that accounts for Mulcahy being nearly caught in Hayes' house which was raided every other week. Diarmuid O'Hegarty, a Corkman, was Director of Organisation at Volunteer headquarters and a really tough character with conspiratorial outlook and agile brain. In Cosgrave's government he was Secretary of the Executive Council. Field Marshal Montgomery was, at that time, a major in the British garrison in Cork and so was General Percival* who had to surrender Singapore to the Japs in the Second War. Amongst the more active leaders of flying columns were the Brennan brothers from Clare, Joe Ring in the West, Lacey and Ryan in Tipperary, Sean Finn of

---

* Percival was a member of the court martial which sentenced Terence McSweeney, Lord Mayor of Cork. McSweeney died in Brixton Prison after seventy-four days on hunger strike (25th October, 1920).

Above: McNamara's funeral: 1922. Below: Casualties at the Custom House: 1921. Photo: Independent Newspapers Ltd.

Above: Collins and an old lady in Co. Cork. Photo: Independent Newspapers Ltd. Below: Generals Mulcahy and McMahon inspect Free State troops.

Limerick (killed in action by the Tans), Liam Hayes of Limerick, T. Hales and T. Barry of Cork, D. Hannigan from Limerick, Michael Hogan and his brother James from Galway. Brian O'Higgins was active in Leix, James Woods from Belfast who was tried for his life and acquitted there. Amongst the best intelligence officers in the Volunteers were Kennedy, Tralee; F. O'Donoghue, Cork; E. Leahy, Limerick. In the peacetime British Army it is said that the most stupid men were picked out for intelligence work, but they soon altered that. Collins looked for the best men for that difficult job and the machine he created worked very well indeed.

18

WHATEVER became of them? Kevin O'Higgins, Minister for Justice, was assassinated in 1927, as was his aged father. The murderers were never brought to justice. My parents died in my home in 1933 within a few weeks of each other. My sister Mary Margaret died in my house in Dublin Castle in 1931. Eileen, who had been injured in the accident which killed Maurice, died in 1955. She had been in the Dail since Stack's time. My sister Bridget died in 1964 of heart failure, in Manchester where she lived, after a lifetime of teaching in Tipperary. My brother Sean and sister Joan still live.

Hurley, Carey and Birmingham served on, got promotion, drew their pensions and died. Foxy-face retired before his time. He feared the new regime and was facing a minor disciplinary charge and dreaded (needlessly) the outcome. He died soon after. His toady Station Sergeant I never saw again. Assistant Commissioner Quinn lived to be about ninety. Constable Nolan, who was carpeted with me before the Commissioner, was accidentally killed by a motorist while on point duty.

Inspector Barleycorn served on under the Free State regime and was promoted. Amusingly enough, he was ordered to report to me on a disciplinary charge, but I had long since forgiven him. Eventually he was retired and lived to a good age. Shortly after Detective Sergeant Johnny Barton discovered that dump of arms, he was shot in the street. Chief Inspector Bruton cleared off to England after the Truce; came back to Dublin and died here. P.C. Connolly, who accused me of studyin', resigned under Article 10 of the Treaty which allowed those people added years of service and pensions.

The Constable with the sparse kit served on and reached a good age, careless of dress as ever, still dodging inspections. Murray and Hetherington, who held the mock funeral to Dalkey for having joined the A.O.H., were allowed to rejoin under the Free State and drew their pensions. Murray was an orderly for a group of us in the castle. He used to say to me: 'They won't stop until they send me to Dalkey again.' Often I got him to tell visitors of the 'funeral' which he did very well. He was immensely tall and of a child-like disposition. The R.I.C. Sergeant McElligott turned Sinn Feiner, became a farmer and lived to a good age. He was anti-Treaty and was imprisoned. Broy joined the Free State Army, rejoined the police, became Commissioner for a few years, and is now retired.

'Count' O'Connor served on and lived to a ripe old age; still good company. Superintendent 'Butt' Brien, after the Castle fired him on pension, disappeared and died of old age. Unobtrusive ever. Beasley, who recited at the party, wrote a monumental two-volume life of Collins and lived to a great age. So did Lord Fitzalan, the last Viceroy, whose arms fill the last half-window of the Chapel Royal. Inspector McFeely, whom the British sacked for not finding the arms that never were, rejoined under the Free State, was made a superintendent, and died of old age.

Detective McNamara, my friend, joined the army as an officer, and in 1922 was killed in a Dublin motor accident. The G-man who described me as a spy for the Pope cleared out to the North. Tim Kennedy, the Kerry I.O., after some close shaves survived the revolution, was anti-Treaty, was in prison during the Civil War and lived to be an old man, dying suddenly. Though we were on opposite sides, we were always good friends.

Austin Stack was anti-Treaty and is now dead. Joe O'Reilly, Collins' faithful courier and disciple, was with him to the end. Shortly before he was killed, Collins said to him: 'How would you like a new boss, Joe?' Joe died of cancer twenty years ago.

Collins, Commander in Chief of the Free State Army, was killed in an ambush in Co. Cork early in the Civil War. A short time before he had attended Arthur Griffith's funeral.

Liam Tobin got high rank in the army, became an officer of the Dail, and retired in ill-health. An invalid for several years, death came to him as a relief. The Bannon brothers, publicans, I never heard of more. Colonel Johnston, D.M.P. Commissioner, served the new Irish regime for a while and retired to England on pension. He told an acquaintance of mine who met him on Brighton Pier that 'Neligan was the one man who disappointed him'.

Inspector-General Byrne of the R.I.C. got a governorship in some island—I hope it did not turn out like Sancho's. General Tudor died in 1965, in Newfoundland, at the ripe age of ninety-three. Inspector-General Smyth I never heard of again after he retired. James McMahon, the school inspector's brother, went to live in England after the Treaty and died there.

Sir John Anderson left with the British, became Governor of Bengal, survived an attempt on his life. Fathering the Anderson shelter, he wound up as Lord Waverley. Curiously enough I was visited by the historian Sir John W. Bennett when he was engaged in writing his biography, but I could not give him any help, knowing very little of his subject. In his book, Bennett seems to have passed over the Castle period in a few lines, but I've seen only extracts from it in a paper.

The Recorder, O'Shaughnessy, served on under the Free State, retired, and was knighted by the British. He visited me once or twice and so did his son-in-law who had such a close escape on his wedding day. I never told them of it, though. Tommy Gay joined the army, retired and went back to the corporation, from which he retired under the age limit. The chest complaint from which he had suffered greatly for years put an end to his life. A widower; his son and daughter are friends of mine. I often tell them of their devoted mother, whom they are too young to remember.

Rory O'Connor was executed during the Civil War as a reprisal for the shooting of a pro-Treaty deputy, Sean Hales. Tom Cullen, light-hearted I.O., was drowned in his native Wicklow while swimming in Lough Dan. Joe Hyland, the faithful taxi-man, still drives one, after a bout of army service. Lord French lived to a good age and never revisited Ireland. General Crozier offered his services to Collins after the Free State was set up, but was refused.

Jimmy Conroy, the one-man column, was in the army and

afterwards emigrated to U.S.A. where he lives still. Tumbleton, who was in the narrow streets called the Dardanelles, was later a detective and is now retired. His pal Hoare was one, too, and is dead. General McCready lived a long time in retirement.

Frank Thornton became an army officer, was wounded during the fighting after the Truce. Later he managed an insurance company and died in 1965, aged seventy-three. His contact in the Auxies disappeared from here, and I do not know anything further of him, though at his request I gave him a letter mentioning his service, which might be useful. Old Superintendent Purcell, who hated to see me in his office, died of old age, still convinced that money was my object in visiting Broy.

The old Sergeant who woke up with Victoria's frame around his neck retired under Article 10 and went home to the North. While Broy was in Arbour Hill Prison, this man visited him and brought him a bottle of whiskey. 'Did you hear about the so-and-so Neligan?' he asked Broy, who was sure he was going to announce my death, as he knew nothing of me since his arrest. 'No, what's happened him?' 'He joined the secret service,' was the reply, 'Maybe to betray them!' Duncan, the Detective Sergeant who was so nearly getting shot, cleared out after the Treaty and is dead.

Alderman Cole, whose premises I watched while the forbidden Dail met in his store, lived to a great age. Years afterwards I was at a party in his house, but did not bother telling him of the incident. The British never suspected him of political leanings or sympathies. R. C. Barton, whose rescue was attempted, still lives and is a great age. His relative Erskine Childers was executed by the Free State for possession of arms. It has been said that he was a British agent here. This is not true. Colonel Winter is dead. Mayem, the British agent, is dead. So are Sir Hamar Greenwood and Cope. Guilfoyle, whom Mayem arrested, still lives and prospers, so does Caldwell who was with him that day. Mayem died in England.

Tommy Barry of Cork is still going strong, like Dan Breen, the one-man Tipperary column. Liam Lynch was shot in the Civil War, in which he took the anti-Treaty side. Miss McGrane, in whose flat Broy's papers were captured, is living in Dublin, the widow of a distinguished medical man. She suffered imprisonment at the time of the raid.

Chief Inspector Supple stuck it out until pension time, and lived to be an old man, in spite of the dire warning he received at the time of Broy's arrest. We did however run into him again. One day during the Truce, Broy, McNamara and I were searching a garage containing stolen British military cars. Broy told us that Supple, now on pension, lived nearby. We decided to take a 'rise' out of him and sent a man to his door who accused him of stealing British Army cars, also that his name was not Supple but Archibald. He was brought to the garage volubly protesting and released after a few minutes. Later I saw him craning his neck when we were leaving in a car. When he saw us he knew it was only a joke.

Sergeant Beggs, the English D.M.P. man, served on after the Treaty, was promoted Inspector, and died while serving. Most of the non-political G-men served on under the Free State. Detective Fenton, who was forever quarrelling, approached me about rejoining, but I advised him against it. Later he became a debt-collector and struck a man who could not pay, thereby narrowly escaping a prison sentence. After that he disappeared. Larry O'Neill walked the tight-rope between the rival armies and died of old age.

Dan Breen is still to the good. He is another who stood by me in dark days.

Tim Healy became the first Governor-General of the Free State and died at a good age, sharp-tongued still. When Cope left Ireland, the higher-ups in the British Civil Service regarded him with no friendly eye. They said he had turned Sinn Feiner! Lloyd George, however, did not neglect his protégé; he gave him a nice job in charge of Welsh collieries and a knighthood. He is now dead. Since then, people on both sides have sought to paint Cope as a regular Machiavelli. That is ridiculous. He was a good public servant. The only difference between him and the other rulers in the Castle was that he saw that the regime was finished and saw it a long time before they did.

The Major I never saw again. When in London in 1921 I visited the Captain at his flat. Count Sévigné shot himself in a

London hotel. Suicide is a secret-service man's occupational disease. After he'd left here he worked for the Northern Ireland Government for a while.

Constable Fitzmaurice I never saw again after that awful day on the Dublin quays. Charley Dalton and his brother Emmet still live. Both served in the army. Dan McDonnell, who was my liaison in Dun Laoghaire, served in the army also and is now retired. I am his daughter's godfather. Billy Walsh, the local O.C., is dead. He being a bookmaker, I'd often betted with him, always on the wrong one! At racing I couldn't win an argument with a dummy.

Sergeant Sullivan wound up his career as an inspector and died of old age, discreet to the end. The red-haired man at Foxrock was, I think, killed during the Civil War, in which he took the anti-Treaty side. The ex-Sergeant-Major, the courier and the tea-planter disappeared. McIntosh, who used to go raiding with the Auxies and who was frightened by the shooting of Cariot, was killed in a drunken brawl, bellicose as ever. Miss McDermott of the Greystones Grand Hotel is now dead.

Mike Noyk, solicitor, was a very old man when he died in 1967. Tommy Gay came to Oriel House during the Truce looking for a loan of a car to bring his wife to a maternity hospital. A taxi strike was in progress in Dublin, and a car or an ambulance could not be got for love or money. He asked the officer in charge of transport, telling him of the circumstances. He was refused. The best car there was reserved for an officer who wanted to go to the theatre where he was the cynosure of all eyes every night, being rigged in full Free State Army uniform with gold braid, Sam Browne belt and all the trimmings. Poor Gay was horrified at such callousness. So was I. 'Wait,' I told him. 'When that popinjay leaves we'll fix you up.' So it was done. We brought the poor little lady to Holles Street Hospital where she died in a few days.

A wonderful spirit of comradeship existed in those terrible days, but sorry I am to say that it did not survive the Truce. Instead we had selfishness, jealousy and a large number of swollen heads. It is quite true, of course, that the character of some of our best men did not deteriorate, but those who were meant by nature to be small showed their true form; they could not stand success, which to some is more damaging than failure.

One of the most staunch of the old I.R.B. men was Sean McGarry, a silent Dublin man. His sister had married an Englishman named Billy Mombrum, who ran an electrical firm in Dublin. McGarry had recruited Mombrum to import warlike stores under the guise of legitimate supplies. This went on for a long time. Eventually, however, the British perhaps were tipped off. Billy was arrested and questioned by a British Intelligence officer. This officer's report eventually found its way to McGarry via a British G.H.Q. employee who sought a little easy money. McGarry afterwards had it framed on his wall. It said: 'This man Mombrum says he is British and a loyal subject but he must be a bad type, for he is Sean McGarry's brother-in-law.'

Those warlike stores were carted by a Volunteer named Daner with an old horse and dray from the North Wall to a secret dump. This was a very dangerous job in those days. One day, in a blinding snow storm, Daner walked with the old horse by the head when there was a bump and the animal stopped. Daner went back and found a poor Jewish pedlar lying under one of the wheels. With the aid of passers-by, the poor fellow was lifted on to the cart and brought to hospital where he died. Daner at the hospital had to give his own name. Some days afterwards he was visited by the dead man's son who demanded compensation. He said he would refer the matter to his employers. So he did.

In the dump, which was manned by some very tough characters, he patiently explained what had happened, adding that the son now sought redress. The answer was soon forthcoming: 'Bring him in here an' we'll plug him.' The next time the son sought Daner he looked in vain.

Daner's old horse survived the revolution but an unhappy fate was reserved for it; his master was suspected of continuing his activities during the Civil War. His opponents broke into the stable and shot the horse. This must surely be the only case in history where a horse had the wrong politics. One day, I told this story to a lot of senior Civil Servants. They were afraid to laugh, thinking there was an allegorical catch to it! Civil Servants have to be very cautious, knowing well on which side their bread is buttered.

I have referred above to the subsequent career of Kennedy, the

Kerry intelligence officer. The position was that he had entered into a secret pact with an officer of the R.I.C. who was willing to give information through him to the Volunteers. This continued for a time until the officer left Kerry. He told Kennedy that a man in the barracks would continue to work for them, and that he could be trusted. This arrangement worked for a time. Kennedy came off the Dublin train one night in Tralee and was on his way home when an R.I.C. man who was not in the swim beckoned him to come down a dark lane. 'Watch out for yourself!' he told Kennedy, 'the man you are in touch with is a wrong one.' This was straight from the horse's mouth. Kennedy went on the run that night and was not at home when armed men with blackened faces raided his lodgings. Sad to relate, that R.I.C. man who warned Kennedy was shot after the Truce, for no reason other than that he had stayed on in the force. The man who shot him had suffered severely from the Black and Tans and of course knew nothing of the incident related above.

Miss Hoey, whose presence of mind and quick thinking saved Collins, is dead. So is G. O'Sullivan, the Adjutant-General who lunched with Collins that day when he said there was something wrong in his secret Mary Street office. O'Sullivan, a Cork man, had been a teacher in his youth, continued as A.G. of the army, and became a barrister. Of those most active then, alas, few are left now.

Tom Ennis, who so narrowly escaped death at the Custom House fire, attained the rank of General in the army, was accidentally wounded (in the same leg) during the Civil War, fell into health so bad that death was a relief. He was, I think, the most unassuming man I've ever met.

In 1932, I received a letter from an Englishmen whom I had known in 1920 in the secret service: 'Dear David, I saw in *The Times* today that you have lost your job. I can only hope that things are not as bad as they say. It is too bad that the people for whom you risked all have treated you so badly. I enclose £10. Please buy me some Sweep tickets with it.' So I come to the end of my story, at least to that part of which I am free to speak.

If anyone asked me was it worth while: would I go through it again: I should answer No. Certainly I do not regret, and shall always look back with affection on my friendship with Michael Collins whose terrific ability and dynamic energy ended so pitiably with a bullet through the head on the side of the road.

I cannot write now of my later association with another great man, Kevin O'Higgins, whose end was similar. Him, too, I remember with love, affection and grief.

It was well said: Revolution devours her own children.

NOTES

The 1916 Rebellion

This rising against British rule in Ireland was started at Easter 1916 and was confined to Dublin. The leaders were two brothers named Pearse, Patrick H. and Willie. Patrick H. was a poet and schoolmaster; T. McDonagh, another poet; Tom Clarke, an aged Fenian who had survived years in British dungeons, often in solitary confinement; Major McBride, who had fought on the side of the Boers; O'Rahilly and Kent, ardent fighters; James Connolly, a radical labour leader; and others of a like way of thinking.

After some days, they were surrounded by superior British forces with artillery and surrendered.

Kitchener, head of the British War Department, sent over General Maxwell, a Scot, to subdue the rebellion. All those who surrendered and hundreds of suspects were arrested, the leaders being executed and the rest deported to Great Britain. Earlier, Kitchener had refused Redmond's offer of Irish troops to be officered by Irishmen under an Irish flag to fight the Germans. Anyway, thousands of Irish had joined the British Army.

When they rose, Pearse and his companions did not have the support of five per cent of the Irish but the execution of those gallant men brought quickly an amazing overwhelming sympathy from the populace.

Before his death, Pearse had foretold exactly that: 'We shall fail,' he said, 'but other men will follow us and succeed.' Though the rising was to all intents and purposes an abject failure, it was followed almost immediately by a resurgence of revolutionary activity which soon burst into a regular war. The prison camps served to an extent as war colleges for the inmates; none of them emerged more loyal to England, but the very opposite.

For two or three years, suffering from terrible casualties in France, the British had been toying with the idea of conscripting the manhood of Ireland for cannon-fodder, and if one thing were needed to consolidate opposition to them it was a renewal of the

SC–F*

threat. This duly arrived and not alone did it fail, but actually drove the potential victims into the arms of Sinn Fein. It is true that a lot of those men faded out later when no longer threatened, being reluctant warriors in any cause!

Sinn Fein

These Gaelic words can be translated freely to mean 'ourselves alone'. An anti-British political movement which in its infancy had but a handful of adherents, it quickly became a formidable national organisation. Out of its ranks came the manpower for the Volunteers and an apparatus of national resurgence, such as was never seen in Ireland before.

Dail Eireann: The Irish Parliament

The Sinn Fein organisation, having decided earlier that its elected M.P.s should not attend the British House of Commons, contested almost every election in Ireland, finally, in 1918 it swept the country. They gained seventy-three seats while the Unionists (pro-British) retained twenty-six, twenty-five of which were in north-east Ulster. Thereby, Redmond's Party, which had held sway for many years, received a fatal blow. Of the Sinn Fein members elected, thirty-six were in prison, three were compulsory exiles and the remainder 'on the run', i.e. evading arrest. In January 1919, those available met at the Dublin Mansion House and set up Dail Eireann. The roll was called and the Clerk replied to a number of names: 'Fe ghlas ag Gallaibh', i.e. 'imprisoned by the English'. Cathal Brugha, the son of an Englishman like the Pearses, presided over the sitting with dignity. A famous fighter, he had refused to surrender in 1916, though gravely wounded. He was killed in the Civil War in 1922.

A Ministry was appointed, a Declaration of Independence passed unanimously. Thus was set in motion a native Government in opposition to the Castle regime, which had governed Ireland for seven hundred years.

Law courts were set up in 1919 and did nearly all the business; the British judges sitting in empty courts The new courts, whose members were unpaid, handled affairs with commendable expedition as they had no fees to collect and nothing to gain through

170

prolonged litigation. The new regime had no prisons but sentenced malefactors to work for poor farmers. They stayed put too, as they stood a good chance of being shot otherwise. The British, of course, did not take all this lying down, but warred continually against the rival regime. That is the best of having an Empire; you get plenty of experience in handling outbreaks!

The Dail appointed delegates under Sean T. O'Kelly who tried in vain to get a hearing at the Peace Conference in Paris. President Wilson turned them down flat: so did the French 'Tiger' Clemenceau, whose mentor was Lloyd George. Wilson was anti-Irish and hated Judge Coholan, an Irish judge in U.S.A. who led the Sinn Fein movement there. Wilson's administration was thoroughly hostile to the Irish revolution and this manifested itself in many ways inimical to the Irish. The fact that they had attempted to obtain German aid gave him a useful handle against them.

The Irish in America

With Coholan, one of the greatest leaders of the Irish in U.S.A. was John Devoy (1842–1928), who had seen the inside of many British dungeons and been transported to the Antipodes for revolutionary activity years earlier. This dedicated rebel, through the Irish Republican Brotherhood (called Clan na Gael in U.S.A.), financed the 1916 rising, negotiated with the German Government for arms and was a kingpin in anti-British circles up to 1921. Irish people in America and their descendants gave vast sums of hard-earned money to finance the struggle and it would be just to state that but for them it could not have succeeded. Devoy's efforts to obtain arms, though, were defeated by the work of a British spy in the office of the German Minister to U.S.A. Devoy lived to an advanced age and the Free State Government of Cosgrave brought his remains to lie in Irish earth. Full military honours were paid at the funeral. No man deserved them better.

The Irish Republican Brotherhood: The Fenians

This secret oath-bound revolutionary body was founded by Stephens and Luby in 1858. O'Donovan Rossa (1831–1915) was one of its leaders and he said he would employ 'dynamite, Greek fire or hell fire if it could be had to drive the British out of Ireland'. For these sentiments and revolutionary activity he served very many years in British dungeons and for much of that time he was chained to the wall like a dog. A rock of granite in Dublin commemorates this iron man whose body was brought back to Ireland from U.S.A. The I.R.B. tried various schemes to oust the British, including a rising and a campaign of dynamiting, but all failed. Though more or less moribund for years, the organisation kept the spark of revolution alive. Tom Clarke, one of its oldest members also like Rossa, an ex-convict was one of the leaders of the 1916 rising and was executed later. Though the British espionage did not actually penetrate the I.R.B. in Ireland, their political police had a good idea of their identity by observing their meeting-places and picking up hints here and there.

The G-men

The Dublin Metropolitan Police area was divided into Divisions A, B, C, D, E and F. The detective division was therefore known as G. The British Government in Ireland organised the G-men at the time of the Fenians to combat that body. Members were drawn from the uniformed force and they served their British masters well. After the collapse of the 1916 rising, the G-men picked out the leaders for court martial and deportation. This excited the wrath of Michael Collins, who on his release from prison started to reorganise both the I.R.B. and the I.R.A. The G-men got ready to resume their espionage but several were summarily shot and those responsible escaped arrest. Also, Collins organised sympathisers in their ranks and turned the machine against itself. This was a body-blow for the British and one from which they did not recover.

The Royal Irish Constabulary (1836–1921)

This body was founded in 1836 by Sir Robert Peel. Hence the nicknames Bobbies and Peelers. Their headquarters was in Dublin Castle and they policed all Ireland except the Dublin area. The R.I.C. was organised somewhat on military lines and were armed with a light carbine or rifle. Their stations, generally comprising a sergeant and a few men, were dotted through the country, generally strategically near cross-roads and very little escaped the force as they were drawn from the people and understood their ways. At the same time, it would not be correct to describe them as a fighting force: they had neither the strength nor the armament to take on anything larger than a village riot. Old Birrell, one time British Chief Officer in Ireland, once said that the R.I.C. had Ireland under a microscope and he was not far wrong. However, the underground methods of the I.R.A. together with the boycotting of the R.I.C. cramped their usefulness. Also, as the revolution progressed they had to withdraw into large towns, thereby abandoning large tracts of country to the rebels. This, with the breakdown of the British legal machine, was the beginning of the end for British rule. It was in an endeavour to combat that situation that the British recruited the Black and Tans and Auxiliaries. Many R.I.C. helped the rebels in various ways.

The Black and Tans (1920–21)
   When the British soldiers and R.I.C. were losing the struggle against the I.R.A. the British decided to augment them. Posters appeared in all Unemployment Exchanges in Great Britain seeking recruits for the R.I.C. whose ranks had been decimated by attacks and resignations. Thousands of ex-soldiers responded to the appeal. As police uniforms were scarce, the recruits were dressed in a motley garb of khaki and blue. This truly suited their character for they were neither police nor soldiers. A well-known pack of hounds in Tipperary is known as the Black and Tans (after the colour of the animals) and some wit so called the new arrivals. The name stuck. The Tans were distributed throughout the country and soon set up a reign of terror, that being their *raison d'être*. No one, combatant or otherwise, was safe from them and they stole everything they could lay hands on. It is likely that they were instrumental in ending British rule here and their doings horrified even the Unionists in Britain. A great British newspaper, *The Manchester Guardian* headed the criticism, also *The Daily News*. Most hostile to the Irish was *The Morning Post*.

The Auxiliaries (1920–21)

This corps consisted of British ex-army officers and the notion of organising them was said to be Churchill's. However that may be, his government recruited them. Totalling about eight or nine hundred and split up into companies of about fifty, they were a really tough mob. Far more dangerous and intelligent than the Tans they, too, created a reign of terror. They burned Cork city, the third largest in Ireland and assassinated two of the leaders of the Dublin I.R.A. whilst their prisoners. Leaving with the British, they joined the Palestine Police, then under British mandate. They did not last long there either. Anyone anxious to follow up the Auxies should read their ex-leader's book: *Ireland For Ever* by Brigadier-General Crozier, an English officer who was fired for trying to enforce discipline on this unruly formation.

The Irish Republican Army, originally named The Irish Volunteers

An underground revolutionary force organised in regular army fashion: all members except for a handful were unpaid: in fact each individual *paid* for his arms and equipment. This body carried on the struggle against the British in 1916 and until the Truce in 1921. Great leaders were Brugha, Barry, Lynch, Ennis, Collins, Mulcahy, McMahon, McKee, Breen, Treacy, Daly, McKeon, Moylan and Traynor.

Arthur Griffith (1871–1922)

Of Northern Irish ancestry, Griffith lived in Dublin for most of his life and had been always a Nationalist. A journalist, he made a meagre living out of little propaganda papers which few read. It would not be an exaggeration to say that he existed very near the poverty line but wanted little from life. Hardly a believer in physical force, he endured many terms in prison. Actually he was released by the British to take part in peace talks. He had formed a great friendship with Collins and both of them signed the Treaty with the British in November 1921. Griffith was a man of noble mind and great character. His name will be forever linked with that of Collins. He died of a broken heart in 1922, a few weeks before the death of Collins. Thus was Ireland deprived of two of her greatest leaders.

Michael Collins (1890–1922)

A poor farmer's son born near Clonakilty, Co. Cork, when his father was aged seventy-five years. Joined the British Civil Service in London as a boy and was later employed in clerical work in that city. Returned to Dublin in January 1916 and participated in the rebellion against the British in April of that year, fighting in the rebel headquarters at the G.P.O. Dublin as a captain. Collins was imprisoned in Frongoch, Wales, with 1,800 other rebels until the general amnesty of prisoners on Christmas Day, 1916, when he went 'on the run' in Dublin. He became a leading member of the Irish Volunteers and had been since his London days a member of the Irish Republican Brotherhood. Later he was a member of its Supreme Council. Collins immediately prepared to renew the struggle against the British who had beaten down the rebellion and executed the seven signatories of the manifesto inaugurating it together with other leaders.

From his experience in the rebellion, Collins correctly concluded that an open fight against the superior British forces did not have a chance, so he prepared for an underground war. A man of daemonic energy and ability, he first decided on wiping out the British intelligence system, which many times in the past had beaten the Irish. Therefore he initiated an Intelligence Corps which sought out and shot the British agents in the police and military forces, so blinding the enemy. He managed to evade arrest by leading an underground life and eventually in 1921 the British Government sought a Truce.

Collins against his will, was sent to London in that year to carry on negotiations with Lloyd George, the British Premier: Stack and Brugha refused to go. A Peace Treaty was signed in London in November of that year. After prolonged debates in the Dail (Irish Parliament) the Treaty was ratified by a majority of seven votes. Collins and Griffith formed a provisional government and fought a Civil War with Irish opponents of the Treaty. Collins, by then Commander-in-Chief of the Pro-Treaty Army was killed by the anti-Treaty forces in an ambush in his native county in 1922, but by that time the native Irish Government had become firmly established, though the country had been torn to pieces and many lives lost.

William T. Cosgrave

Dublin born, Cosgrave was a Sinn Feiner from youth. He participated in the 1916 rising and was imprisoned. A member of the Dublin Corporation, he became a minister in the proscribed Dail and in the Provisional Government set up by the pro-Treaty members of the Dail. On the death of Griffith, he assumed leadership of the government and did great work restoring order and building up a new State out of the ruins. He lived to an advanced age, having retired some years previously.

General Mulcahy

Born in Waterford, Mulcahy was a rebel all his life. Employed as a Post Office technician until the British sacked him he soon reached high rank in the rebel army, being Chief of Staff during the struggle. With Tom Ashe and a column he fought a miniature battle against strong forces of R.I.C. near Ashbourne, Co. Meath, in 1916 at the end of which the surviving police surrendered. Always a jump ahead of British raiding parties he had some narrow escapes. After the death of Collins he became Commander-in-Chief of the Free State Army, then a Minister, then an T.D. and is now retired. A quiet-spoken man, rather withdrawn in manner, he has plenty of steel in his make-up and rendered great service to the revolution and to the infant State.

Eamonn de Valera

This man was born in the U.S.A. in 1882. Reared by relatives in Co. Limerick, he was in his youth a teacher. He took part in the 1916 rising and was elected to the Dail by Clare which remained faithful to him for years. He went to the U.S.A. in 1919, returning in December 1920. He met Lloyd George in earlier peace talks in July 1921 but was not present at the final stage. Leader of the anti-Treaty party, though taking no part in the fighting after the Treaty, he entered the Dail in 1927, gaining power in 1932. Elected President of the State in 1959 he still (1968) holds that office.

Kevin O'Higgins (1892-1927)

The noblest Roman of them all! Son of a doctor in the Irish

176

Midlands, O'Higgins was intended for the Church. On leaving the seminary, he studied law and was soon caught up in the revolutionary movement. Elected a member of the first Dail, he soon came to the front. A most logical and incisive thinker and speaker, he had qualities of realism and moral courage rare in Ireland or in any other place. In favour of the Treaty, he became Minister for Justice and a leading figure in Cosgrave's government. He set about restoring the rule of law and order. He and his fellow-Minister P. McGilligan did useful work in London at the Imperial Conference in 1926, notably in the full emancipation of the dominions which was enshrined in the Statute of Westminster *circa* 1931. O'Higgins had a bitter tongue with which he habitually lashed his opponents and pointed out in no uncertain manner their shortcomings. This made him their most hated enemy. He was murdered by gunmen on his way to Mass near Dublin in 1927. The assassins were never brought to justice. Churchill described him as 'A figure from the antique cast in bronze.' It is too early yet to assess the real stature of this great man, but one can be certain that future historians will give him his rightful place in Irish history, amongst the greatest of her gallant sons.

The Orangemen

This society dates from 1795 and is extreme Protestant Irish Conservative. Their patron 'Saint' is Dutch William who seized the throne from his father-in-law James. William, though unsuccessful in battle heretofore, with the aid of more Catholics than Orangemen won the battle of the Boyne against James in 1690. William had good generals, including Schomberg and Ginkel. James's army was composed of English, Irish and Scots. Legend has it that James told a witty lady that his army ran away and she replied: 'If that is so your Majesty won the race!'

It has often been the misfortune of the Irish to fall for smooth-talking con men but the worst of all was James. In the Gaelic language he is known by an unprintable epithet which he deserves richly. The Orangemen, descendants of English and Scots planters, have always had a pathological fear and hatred of their Catholic countrymen and this exists to this day. Following the

177

Imperial Roman adage, 'Divide and Conquer', the British have availed themselves of this mentality through the ages.

Randolph Churchill, M.P. (father of Winston), said long ago: 'The Orange card is the one to play' and it has been played ever since.

The Boundary Commission

In pursuance of a clause in the Treaty of 1921, a Boundary Commission was set up to delimit the boundary between Carson's supporters and the rest of Ireland. The dice were loaded. Thus we have an unnatural frontier in this little island and one likely to remain so far as can be seen. In his youth, when a member of Asquith's government, Winston Churchill was prepared to use force to bring the Orangemen to heel. This gave rise to the Curragh Mutiny when senior British officers refused to serve 'against Ulster'. This affair was instigated by a leading Orange sympathiser at the War Office, Sir H. Wilson. The Orangemen, led by Carson and Craig, armed themselves with arms bought from the Kaiser's country. The British Government put the matter on the long finger as the First World War broke out. The arming of the Orangemen stimulated a like movement in Dublin and led to the formation of the Irish Volunteers with the result to be seen. That the revolt of the Orangemen should lead to the British losing twenty-six counties of Ireland is surely one of the ironies of history!

Sir John Anderson

A Scot, Anderson was a keyman in the Dublin Castle regime. Leaving with the British in 1922 he became Governor of Bengal, surviving an attempted assassination. Raised to the Peerage as Lord Waverley, he was a Cabinet Minister in London and is now dead.

Sir Andrew Cope

An Englishman, polite and urbane, he is supposed to have commenced his official life as a Customs official and was said to be a protégé of Lloyd George. With Anderson, he was a leader of the Castle regime. Cope took a leading part in peace talks with the

178

Irish under the direct instructions of Lloyd George. After the Treaty he left the Civil Service and obtained a high position in the Welsh collieries (do we see Lloyd George's hand here?) and a Knighthood. He is now dead.

Dublin Castle

The centre of British rule in Ireland up to 1922, it was the Irish Bastille. Said to have been founded by King John of Magna Carta fame, it is a shapeless medley of buildings. The Castle regime was notorious for its nourishment of informers through the ages and paid out millions to them. I do not suppose that informers are popular anywhere, but a terrible odium attached to them in Ireland, where memories are long indeed. At one time the Castle maintained a home for them in Dublin to save their lives. In my presence an old policeman said of a colleague: 'Sure he couldn't be good, his great-grandfather was reared in the informers' home!'

The Active Service Unit I.R.A.

This was a formation of about fifty I.R.A. men who received a small subsistence salary and were fully employed on warlike activities, operating in Dublin and its environs. Daly and Leonard were leaders.

The Squad

Consisted of about twelve men primarily responsible to Collins. The squad engaged in executing informers and enemy agents and in counter-espionage. Tobin, Cullen and Thornton were leaders. They were paid like the A.S.U.

King George's Speech in Belfast

King George opened the Six Counties Parliament on the 22nd June, 1921. That day he spoke in Belfast.

'I speak from a full heart when I pray that my coming to Ireland may prove to be the first step towards the end of strife among her people, whatever their race or creed. . . . The future lies in the hands of the Irish people themselves . . .'

The better part of the speech was the King's own. A separate government now existed in the Six Counties area and this put paid to the hopes of an all-Irish republic. It was therefore out of the question that any Dublin delegation could now secure a republic for the whole of Ireland and Collins and Griffith and our whole Cabinet knew it. We were not strong enough to beat the British out of Ireland and that was the end of it.

The Sinn Fein Funds

As stated above (pages 77-8), Collins had collected in the Dail Loans £378,858 in Ireland and $5,800,000 in the United States. Of this £25,700 was buried under a concrete floor in Batt O'Connor's house in Dublin.

Following on the split in Sinn Fein, the leaders could not agree as to the division of the balance of these funds. A protracted law suit ensued. One of the fables of Aesop (6th century B.C.) illustrates the result: Two cats found a large lump of cheese but could not agree as to its division. A monkey came along with a pair of scales. They appealed to him. He broke the cheese into two pieces which he put on the scales. As one was heavier, he bit a lump off it. That made it too light and so he continued until the whole had disappeared down his throat.

The whole story cannot yet be told.

Dan Breen and Sean Treacy

Those two men, whose photograph faces page 33, were remarkable characters who would require a book to themselves.

Hailing from County Tipperary, they started the ball rolling after 1916 when, on the 21st January, 1919, they shot two R.I.C. escorting a load of gelignite in Tipperary.

It was but a coincidence that the first meeting of the first Dail took place in Dublin on that day. That this body had not yet sanctioned a state of war with Britain did not trouble them unduly. From that day those two were the most hunted men in Ireland.

Their narrowest escape was in the house of Professor Carolan on the outskirts of Dublin on the night of 11th October, 1920. They were surrounded by British military following on their being shadowed to the house by a British agent. Hearing the ratatat, Breen fired through the hall-door, killing Colonel Smyth and another officer.

Firing from the British became general and in the mêlée Breen fell through a glass roof and was badly injured. Losing sight of Treacy, he crawled through fields all night and finally found refuge in a friendly house, having shot several others of the raiding party on his way out.

As has been told here, Treacy was killed by the British on the 13th October, 1920, in Talbot Street, Dublin, but Breen was never captured. The British shot their host, Carolan, that night.

If I were engaged in a tiger-hunt, I'd pick Breen and Treacy.

The Irish Bulletin

The Sinn Fein publicity machine was very effective. It issued the *Irish Bulletin* beginning in September 1919. This was an underground sheet edited by Desmond Fitzgerald, and for six months by Erskine Childers.

This clandestine organ found its way all over the world and certainly did something to counter British propaganda. Fitzgerald, a gifted and handsome man, was afterwards Minister for External Affairs in Cosgrave's government, and was a devoted rebel as well as a charming fellow. He is now dead.

Childers, an able man and author of a pre-1914 novel, *The Riddle of the Sands*, took a leading part against Collins and against the Treaty. He was executed by the Free State Government during the Civil War in November 1922.

The Reward for Collins

As I have mentioned on page 135, the head of the British secret service in Dublin offered me £10,000 if I could bring about the capture of Collins.

Some of those here who have benefited so much by the work of Collins, and for whom the British did not offer one penny reward, would like to throw doubt on this.

One man telephoned to me and asked me had I any proof of the offer! I answered 'no', but perhaps I should have asked the

English officer to go before a notary, so that I could have the proof, but that did not strike me at the time.

I can assure those unbelieving 'patriots', who are so plentiful here nowadays, that it is true and not only that but I am convinced that anyone offering the British Collins' head in 1920–21, could have named his own reward. The British spend money like water when vital interests are at stake and have always done so.

A British Officer's View of the Volunteers

General Sir H. Lawson, K.C.B., came to Ireland in 1920 to enquire into the Irish Rebel Army. His findings were published in the British press of 30th December, 1920:

> 'The Captains . . . appear to have been . . . as a class sincere and single-minded idealists, highly religious for the most part and often with an almost religious sense of duty to their country. They fought against drunkenness and self-indulgence and it is no exaggeration to say that they represented all that was best in the countryside.'

For this quotation I am indebted to Shaw Desmond in his book *The Drama of Sinn Fein* (William Collins Sons & Co., 1923).

Paudeen O'Keeffe

A man of small stature, this devoted rebel had in his character the granite of his native hills on the Cork-Kerry border. Dismissed from the Post Office after 1916 for refusing to take the oath of allegiance to the British, he was appointed Secretary of Sinn Fein in 1919. A devoted follower and friend of Collins, he was the best type of revolutionary—all for the cause—nothing for self. Two English newspaper reporters, with pencils poised, interviewed him in 1919 and asked what Ireland sought. He replied with commendable brevity: 'Vengeance, by Christ!'

In the Civil War in 1922 he took the unwanted job of Governor of Mountjoy prison, where he was visited by Madame Maud Gonne McBride (who was on the other side of the fence). She told him that the prisoners would escape from his custody. 'Madame', says he: 'nothing escapes from here except gas!' and nothing did.

Collins and the Pubs

Collins used public-houses in Dublin as meeting places with his agents. This lent colour to lies put out by his political enemies in 1922 that he was a drunkard. These lies have got a long start. Nothing could be further from the truth and the worst of it is that those who spread the lies knew that they were lies. The public-houses in question were: L. Devlin's in Parnell Street, J. Kirwan's in Mary Street, Phil Shanahan's at the North Wall and several others. The owners were sympathisers and the staffs (known amusingly enough as grocer's curates) were nearly all Volunteers. Collins met there prison warders, friendly R.I.C., 'G' men, seamen and others actively engaged in underground work for him. Nearly all 'curates' in Dublin were Volunteers and good types of youths from the provinces.

In all my meetings with Collins I never saw him drink anything except a glass of sherry. I don't suppose this statement will silence the calumniators, who thought it wonderful to be considered greater patriots than Michael Collins, and also uncanonised saints! As Griffith said before he died: 'such hypocrisy is damnable'.

INDEX

186

187